PLAYS 1

TESTAMENT
Tristan Bernays

SAVE + QUIT
Sophia Leuner

WRETCH
Rebecca Walker

THIS MUST BE THE PLACE
Brad Birch & Kenneth Emson

MAISIE SAYS SHE LOVES ME
Jimmy Osborne

PLAYS FROM VAULT 2

TESTAMENT
Tristan Bernays

SAVE + QUIT
Sophia Leuner

WRETCH
Rebecca Walker

THIS MUST BE THE PLACE
Brad Birch & Kenneth Emson

MAISIE SAYS SHE LOVES ME
Jimmy Osborne

NICK HERN BOOKS
London
www.nickhernbooks.co.uk

A Nick Hern Book

Plays from VAULT 2 first published in Great Britain in 2017 as a paperback original by Nick Hern Books Limited, The Glasshouse, 49a Goldhawk Road, London W12 8QP, in association with VAULT Festival

Testament copyright © 2017 Tristan Bernays
Save + Quit copyright © 2017 Sophia Leuner
Wretch copyright © 2017 Rebecca Walker
This Must Be the Place copyright © 2017 Brad Birch, Kenneth Emson
Maisie Says She Loves Me copyright © 2017 Jimmy Osborne

The authors have asserted their moral rights

Cover design by Thomas K Shannon

Designed and typeset by Nick Hern Books, London
Printed and bound in Great Britain by Mimeo Ltd, Huntingdon, Cambridgeshire PE29 6XX

A CIP catalogue record for this book is available from the British Library

ISBN 978 1 84842 656 6

Woodland
CARBON
www.woodlandcarbon.co.uk
NICK HERN BOOKS
Printed on Carbon Captured paper

Contents

Welcome (Back) to VAULT

2017 marks the fifth time the VAULT Festival has taken over the tunnels beneath Waterloo Station, transforming them into a hub for artists and audiences to explore the very best in exciting, innovative and risky creative arts projects. A seemingly impossible idea we had in late 2011 has grown, through the hard work of hundreds of people, into an annual celebration that London has embraced with an unruly and humbling passion.

From theatre and comedy to film and late-night entertainment, our goal with VAULT remains to create a vibrant underworld in which daring performers can find intrepid audiences without the financial and structural burdens that too often accompany any artistic enterprise.

It takes courage to come to these bizarre tunnels – now a fantastic year-round venue known as The Vaults – and present something for all to see. If the plays included in this collection are anything to go by, courage is not in short supply among the crop of artists that we are immensely proud to be hosting this year.

This volume represents just a fraction of the wealth of talent lurking below the surface of our city, and it's with great pleasure that we present it to you.

Mat Burt, Andy George & Tim Wilson
VAULT Festival Directors

Biographies

TRISTAN BERNAYS

Tristan is a writer and performer from London. He trained at the University of Bristol and LAMDA. His work has been performed at Soho Theatre, Bush Theatre, National Theatre Studio, Roundhouse and Southwark Playhouse.

His new play *Boudica* will be produced at Shakespeare's Globe in September 2017 as part of Emma Rice's Summer of Love season.

His show *Teddy* won Best New Musical at the 2016 Off West End Awards, and he is a member of Bush Theatre's Emerging Writers' Group 2016/17.

Credits include *Frankenstein* (Watermill Theatre/Wilton's Musical Hall; dir: Eleanor Rhode); *Teddy* (Southwark Playhouse; dir: Eleanor Rhode); *The Bread & The Beer* (Soho Theatre/UK tour; dir: Sophie Larsmon); *Coffin* (King's Head Theatre; dir: Oliver Rose).

www.tristanbernays.com / @tristanbernays

SOPHIA LEUNER

Sophia Leuner wrote the first half of *Save + Quit* for the London Student Drama Festival in 2015. While living in Dublin in 2016, she wrote the second half and it was first performed in its entirety at Assembly George Square, Edinburgh Fringe Festival 2016.

She has had short plays produced at the HighTide Festival, the Park Theatre, the Etcetera Theatre and The Cockpit.

Sophia is currently completing her MFA in Dramatic Writing at NYU Tisch.

REBECCA WALKER

Rebecca's debut play *Wretch* was commissioned by theatre company Into The Wolf, and completed a tour of homeless day centres, drug rehab clinics and hostels in 2015, before being produced by Interval Productions in its first theatrical run at VAULT 2017.

She has had short plays produced at The Cockpit, Arcola Theatre, Pleasance Edinburgh, The Vaults, Southwark Playhouse, Bush Theatre, Theatre503 and Tristan Bates Theatre, and is a graduate of the Royal Court's Invitation Group, Young Writers' Programme and the Criterion Theatre's New Writing Group.

BRAD BIRCH

Plays include *The Brink* (Orange Tree); *En Folkefiende* and *The Endless Ocean* (RWCMD); *Even Stillness Breathes Softly Against A Brick Wall* (Soho Theatre); *Tender Bolus* (Royal Exchange); *Gardening for the Unfulfilled and Alienated* (Undeb – and winner of a 2013 Scotsman Edinburgh Fringe First). Brad was the recipient of the 2016 Harold Pinter Commission at the Royal Court.

KENNETH EMSON

Plays include *Rural* (White Bear); *Whispering Happiness* (Tristan Bates); *Our Nobby* (Eastern Angles, touring); *The Peterborough Effect* (Eastern Angles, touring); *England Street* (Oxford Playhouse); *Terrorism* (Bush Theatre). Kenny also writes for TV and film and was nominated for a BAFTA Craft Award in 2016 for his work on *The Last Hours of Laura K*.

JIMMY OSBORNE

Jimmy Osborne is a playwright and screenwriter. He and David Aula co-adapted Ian McEwan's *The Cement Garden*, headlining the London VAULT Festival 2014. *An Empty Seat*, commissioned by The Stephen Joseph Theatre, dealt with cowardice and heroism during the First World War. *The Room Inside*, was selected by the Writers' Guild as part of Playwright's Progress and won a commendation at the Curve Theatre and BBC Writersroom Playwriting Award. *Meat* was staged at Theatre503.

This book went to press before the end of rehearsals and so the texts may differ slightly from the plays as performed.

TESTAMENT

Tristan Bernays

Testament was first performed at VAULT Festival, London, on 22 February 2017, with the following cast:

ISAAC   Tristan Bernays
LOT'S DAUGHTERS   Peta Cornish
                                         Celeste Dodwell
THE THIEF ON THE CROSS   Simon Manyonda
MUSICIAN   Ivy Davies

Director   Lucy Jane Atkinson
Producer   Darius Thompson,
                                         Old Sole Theatre Company
Designer   Verity Johnson
Sound Designer   Mark Sutcliffe
Music   Ivy Davies

'What in me is dark, illumine.'
Paradise Lost, John Milton

Characters

ISAAC
LOT'S DAUGHTERS (M *and* J)
THE THIEF ON THE CROSS

Time

Now

Place

America

Note

A live musician should accompany each short play, and each
piece should be intercut with a song (see Songbook Appendix).

Isaac

A psychiatrist's office.

ISAAC *sits in a chair.*

ISAAC. My father called last week to wish me happy birthday.
It's the first time that he's done it in years. I didn't talk to
him – Jessica, my wife, she – She's the one who – She
thought it might be good to talk to –

So she's the one who spoke to him, which was difficult
because she didn't know I still had a dad. I'd told her that he'd
died years ago and that was all fine, except when this guy rings
up out of the blue and says 'Can I speak to Isaac, please?' And
she's like 'He's not in right now, can I take a message?' and he
says 'Can you tell him his father called?' And she's like 'Okay
– who is this?' and he says 'This is Isaac's father – who is
this?' and she says 'I'm his wife' and he sorta laughs and says
'He never told me that he got married.'

Now most people'd would be like, 'Oh screw you this, this is
bullshit, I – ' Sorry, sorry I don't – I don't usually – swear,
I'm not – Most people would say this is – bullcrap but you
have to understand that my father is very persuasive. He's
got this voice, this sorta rumbly low kinda burr. Very solid
and trustworthy, you know? I didn't inherit it, I've got this
kind of – I sound like a Jewish dentist. It's not a voice that
inspires devotion in others.

So before she could say anything my father began talking
and Jessica listened and by the sounds of it they had quite the
chat. Talked about how long we'd been married and the kids
and pretty soon the two of them are getting on like a house
on fire.

I'm getting this all second hand, you understand – from my
wife – who's layin' into me, asking 'Why?', why I don't
wanna talk to him and she won't quit going at it, won't quit –
even though it is my birthday, I might add, I'm still the –

But I tell her fine, okay, fine. I'll tell you why we don't speak any more.

My mother died when I was very young. That left just my father and I and he raised me all by himself. I don't really remember her. But my father. Jesus, he was – like a rock, just – He had stone-grey hair and smelt of Old Spice. He was a pastor, admired, respected. He was very serious, he – I mean – he wasn't one of those touchy-feely kinda dads, you know, I – I mean you weren't exactly gonna be throwing a football around in the backyard or – or be horsin' around with him or nothin' but – but – I knew that he loved me. Cos I was the only one who could make him smile. Like when I'd – I dunno, I'd come into his study when he was writing one of his sermons and show him like some magic trick I'd been working on or a picture I'd drawn or something – you know like how your kids, they – And he wouldn't just be like 'Oh yeah, that's great, honey, yeah – woo', no, no he – he – He would stop what he was doing and he would sit and watch and his serious face would thaw into this smile that cocked the one side of his mouth and he'd get little crow's feet around his eyes from the smiling and the wrinkling. I was the only one who could make him smile like that. Really smile, like from the – like from the middle, you know? And when he smiled at me like that I could see how much he loved me. And there were two things that he loved more than anything else in this world: me and God.

And then one day God started speaking to him. Yes, yes, I know, I said he was a pastor, that sorta comes with the territory but I don't mean – This wasn't a kind of, you know, 'He's always there when I need him', I mean this was well and truly like 'Abraham, this is God – listen up!' We were having breakfast and he just dropped his coffee cup on the floor, smashed it and I looked up and he was just staring into space, his eyes were like – Like he was looking at something I couldn't see and – And he started smiling and I said,

'What is it, Daddy?'

and he said,

'He just spoke to me.'

'Who?'

'God.'

I hardly saw him after that – I mean he was still at home, still looked after me and carried on working and preaching but he'd go out for hours at a time I don't know where and just – I found him one night in the backyard. I went outside in my pyjamas – I was waiting for him to come tuck me in – and I saw him looking up at the sky at this big, blue black sky fulla stars. It was a big sky, I mean it was – huge, you – And I stood next to him, slid my hand in his and saw him smiling, and I remember thinking – feeling like a real grown-up, being like 'Wow, here I am, up late like a proper grown-up and sharing this moment with my dad!' And then I looked up and I realised – He had no idea I was there. He was miles away. And I say,

'Dad? Daddy?'

and he looks down at me he says,

'Yes, son?'

And I said,

'What ya doing?'

And he was quiet for a moment, then he just smiles and says,

'Just listening. Just listenin' to Him.'

And he goes back to lookin' at the sky and smilin'.

Two weeks later, I wake up in the middle of the night and he's sitting on the edge of my bed, hands resting on his lap and his big dark eyes looking out at me from under his brows. And I'm like,

'Daddy? What's – '

– I can see through my curtains it's still dark outside – and he says,

'It's okay, son, we need to get up. Don't worry, just – get up and get dressed and I'll tell you more on the way.'

So he gets me up and he takes me to the bathroom and I can see he's run a fresh bath and he stands outside the door while I go pee then he peels off my pyjamas and he gets me in the tub and starts scrubbing away at me, real thorough – scrubbing away at me till there's not a speck of dirt left. Then he lifts me out the tub, wraps me up in this big pink towel and starts drying me off, running a brush through it to get out all the knots out. And he leads me back into my bedroom and he's laid out my clothes for me on the bed – my Sunday best – and he begins to dress me, real meticulously like – like he's really focused on the buttons and the laces and – and getting the creases outta the – And it's really strange cos this is the most – attentive he's been with me for some time. Finally, he sits back, looks me up and down and nods to himself like he's happy with how I look. But I notice that for the first time in months he's not smiling.

He takes me downstairs and there's this big sports bag on the kitchen table. And he picks it up and opens the back door and he says,

'Come on.'

He leads me outside, takes my little hand in his and it feels so small – like a tiny little fish – and he walks us up out the back gate and through the fields of long grass out back towards the top of the hill, holding hands the whole way, walking the whole way in silence. And it's not a hard walk but – you know, I'm having to walk four steps for every one of his huge – and I'm starting to get hot and sweaty and a bit breathless but I don't say anything, cos Dad looks so focused and determined and I don't wanna, you know –
I don't wanna –

And we finally get to the top, to this clearing – teenagers used to come up here and smoke and drink, you know, like – but it was empty that night and we can see the whole town glowing under the stars and I remember it looked beautiful, really – Norman Rockwell. People always rose-tint the past, you know? But that night right then it looked – it really looked –

Then he leads me over these rocks in the centre of the clearing, and one of them's fallen over and it's made this kinda table. Like an altar. And picks me up with his big hands and plops me down on the rock so I'm sitting on it with my little legs dangling off the edge. And he crouches down and he looks at me dead in the eyes and he says,

'Isaac. You know Daddy loves you, don't you? You know he loves you very, very much.'

And I knew this was a serious question so I say,

'Yeah, I know that, Daddy.'

And for the first time that night he smiles at me.

Then he says it's really important to do exactly what he tells me to do and I say okay. And I sit there, nice and still like he asks, as he takes a length of brown rope out of the bag and binds my wrists and ankles and lays me flat out on the rock, cradling my head so I don't hit it when I lie down.

And it's cold on the rock, and the ropes are really tight and I need to pee real bad but I don't wanna say nothin' cos I don't wanna upset him. And he looks down at me, his eyes as big and black and empty as the skies above, and he leans down and says in that low rumbly, kinda burr and he says,

'It's okay, son. You're being very brave. I need you to do one more thing. I need you to close your eyes real tight and look away.'

And I don't want him to see me cry – So I just nod and he says,

'Good'

and he leans down and kisses me on the forehead. And I can feel his stubble, smell his Old Spice.

So I close my eyes and look away. I don't know what he's doing and I don't wanna look cos he told me not to but I'm really scared and the ropes hurt and I really need to pee and I turn my head and I open one eye just a crack, just a little bit so I can see what he's doing and I watch him as he reaches into the bag and pulls out a knife.

A long silver hunting knife with a green handle, very sharp and clean. And he turns around and sees me looking straight at him.

He moves very quickly, covers my eyes, pushes me against
the rock and it hurts, it really – I try to say something but my
voice is trapped in my throat, I can't – I can feel his sweat on
his hands and the Old Spice smell and suddenly there's this
cold, sharp point against my – The knife, I can feel it
pushing against my neck shaking, his – breathing, he's trying
to – get himself ready to – to – to push it in – to –

And then it stops. Everything stops. No sound, just a –
ringing in my ears. I can still feel the knife against my neck
but it's stopped shaking. I turn my head, look through his
fingers. And I can see my father just – looking up. And he's
listening again. But it's like no one's there. No one's talking
to him.

I say 'Daddy?' and he blinks and swallows, comes to like
he's waking up and he looks down at me with those big eyes.
And he looks at me for the briefest moment it's like he
doesn't know who the hell I am. And then he finally sees me
and the knife against my neck.

And he very carefully he takes the knife away from my – my
throat and he starts to undo ropes. His hands are sweaty and
shaking, and he gets me back up sitting again and he looks at
me very intensely, like it's the first time he's ever seen me.
I smell something strong and we both look down and there's
a dark patch where I've wet myself. And he suddenly
becomes very embarrassed and looks away. A wind blows
and it's cold – I can feel my penis shrivel – and he steps back
and lets me slide down from the rock. We stand there for a
moment, then he starts packing up the bag and then we set
off again back down the hill to our house, me following
behind this time, not holding hands.

By the time we get back to the kitchen, the sun is coming up.
My father undoes my laces and slips off my soiled clothes
and I let him, then he leaves me standing there half-naked in
the middle of the kitchen, my little penis peeping out from
under the hem of my shirt, as he comes back in with a new
change of underpants and a blanket and he helps me into the
underpants, one leg at a time, and he puts the blanket around
my shoulders then then leads me slowly to the table where
he sits me down at the head of it.

I sit in silence and he moves around the kitchen, opening and closing drawers and cupboards. Then he comes back to the table and puts a bowl and a spoon in front of me, and then fills it with cereal – Cap'n Crunch – and pours cold milk over it. Then he puts the cereal and the milk on the table and sits down next to me. And we sit the two of us in silence, the only sound the crackle of milk on the cereal. And I look at my father. And he looks at me. And I pick up the spoon and dip it in the bowl and begin to eat the cereal.

We just carried on. My father and I. Never talked about it. We shared a table and ate together, but did not speak, not really. The conversation sort of dwindled and dwindled until one day we just – stopped talking. I left for college when I was seventeen, went as far north as I could whilst retaining some semblance of civilisation. That was the last time I saw my father. The last time we even spoke.

I told her all this – Jessica – and she said – She went really quiet for a bit. Then she said 'But – but why would he – I mean, you're his son. He loved you.'

Yes he did. But it turns out he loved God more.

14

Lot's Daughters

A kitchen at Thanksgiving.

Afternoon.

M *and* J *stand smiling.*

M. Thanksgiving's always gonna be hectic round our house.

J. Amen to that.

M. I mean, you got fourteen people round a table with all the kids and the men –

J. Though you'd be hard pressed to find the difference.

M. Oh yes, you'd be hard pressed to – I mean you look at them out there now, in the yard throwin' that pig skin about –

J. You can't tell which is which!

M. That's my Chuck over there 'bout to make a pass – Chuck used play quarterback in college – and then that's her Tom over there, good-lookin' blond on the other side, and her two beautiful boys.

J. Dale and Jonah.

M. And that's my pride and joy over there, my little Billy.

J. He is as big as they come, now.

M. He's gonna be a quarterback someday too, I just know it, I – Here, let me give him a – Billy! Coo-ee!

J. Billy! Billy darlin'!

M. Oh, he's wavin'!

J. Hey Billy!

M. Hey, Billy Bee!

J. You boys playin' nice, now?

M. You enjoyin' the game? Who's winnin'? I said who's – They can't hear us.

J. Can't hear you through the glass.

M. So we got all that lot out there to feed –

J. And then with Tom and Chuck's family and whatnot –

M. It's always gonna be a big order, you know what I mean?

J. 'Less you plan it.

M. 'Less you plan it.

J. We doin' it at hers this year.

M. We doin' it at mine. It was hers last year –

J. Mine last year.

M. – and you did such a beautiful job.

J. Stop!

M. You did!

J. Stop! You are makin' me blush!

M. My sister is the hostess with the mostess – she puts on a spread that'd knock your socks off!

J. Oh now, you stop!

M. You do!

J. We alternate it cos –

M. Well it is like feedin' an army –

J. Only with more casualties!

M. – so we alternate hostin' but we always do it together.

J. The Two Musketeers.

M. The Two Musketeers, that's right!

J. We's a team. Host handles meat and sauces.

M. Back-up does the veggies and the pie.

M & J. And the men does the washin' up after!

J. She's my best friend.

M. She's mine.

J. Always was, growin' up together.

M. We shared a room.

J. In pink.

M. Of course.

J. You remember those Thanksgivin's?

M. Oh Lord, yes I – You think this is busy now?

J. Back then we had aunts and uncles and nieces and nephews and friends and family all piled up high to the rafters –

M. And lookin' out over it all – presidin' over ever'thin' was Mommy and Daddy.

J. They was real pillars of the community.

M. That is it, that is it in a nutshell – 'community'. Our town had a real sense of community spirit. And Mommy and Daddy, they was just such a big part of it.

J. Oh God, yes.

M. Momma useta play organ in church.

J. She looks just like her, I swear.

M. Daddy was Head of the Civic Pride Committee –

J. Useta organise charity events and Fourth o' July parades for the veterans.

M. He just oozed pride for our town outta every pore.

J. You would've too. You'da been real proud to walk around our little town.

M. Not all of it.

J. Oh no – no, no not all of it.

M. Lord, no.

J. There's certain parts o' town you wouldn't walk into if you knew what's good for you.

M. Rough part o' town.

J. There'd be – drinkin' and gamblin' and all sorts o' hell and holler. I tell you, there's more blue lights in that place than there was red.

M. Oh yeah, yeah that was where you'd go for – women.

J. Loose women.

M. But it weren't just women neither.

J. Oh no! There's other reason's you'd go there. If you were – were –

M. Well let's just if we wasn't a landlocked town itta been fulla sailors.

J. I mean – What you choose to do in the privacy of your own home is your own business – but when you are – shakin' in my face –

M. With them bars and parades and whatnot, well then – well then it stops bein' your private business. Stops bein' decent.

J. That's what Daddy was fightin' for. To keep things decent.

M. To keep our town a nice town.

J. He petitioned to the Town Council about it. Him and the Committee – he led it. Put forward their case, very eloquent on why they had to stem this – corrupting influence on the town. And the Council, well they – They gave him the whole 'Thank you for your concern, it's duly noted – '

M. ' – but there's nothing that we can legally do about it. They're not breaking any laws.'

J. And Daddy said if that was the case then their laws were – Pardon my French – a piece of shit not worth the paper they were written on.

M. He was very passionate about it.

J. Swore he'd fight on – and he did.

M. He organised the Committee together for rallies and protests. Momma was there, us too, wavin' our little banners.

J. But after a while others from the Committee –

M. Friends he'd started out with.

J. – they started showin' up less and less. It was too hard for them, see.

M. And Daddy started getting angry with them.

J. He was a passionate man, see.

M. Started calling 'em quitters.

J. Started getting this reputation for bein' high an' mighty.

M. All he's tryna do is raise us –

J. Raise a family good and proper. He's doin' the best he can.

M. They walked out on Daddy. Abandoned him. Nobody'd talk to him. We's the only decent ones left in the whole sordid damn town, Daddy'd say.

J. It was tough.

M. They's difficult times.

J. But you want the rainbow, you gotta put up with the rain.

M. Who said that?

J. Dolly.

M. Amen to that.

J. You like Dolly?

M. Oh we love her, she is jus' the best.

J. The best.

M. 'Workin' 9 to 5'

M & J. 'What a way to make a livin'!'

M. Oh Lord, what are we –

J. That woman is just –

M. Royalty.

J. Genius.

M. She really is, she's just so – strong and good and – When I think about what she went through – as a little girl growin' up – All them hard times and she still just – just –

J. Hey, hey it's okay.

M. I'm sorry, it's silly, I –

J. It's okay.

M. I feel all – I shouldn't be like this –

J. Don't.

M. – in front of a –

J. We don't have to talk none about it if you don't –

M. No, no, I'm okay, I'm okay, I just – 's just difficult to know – 'xactly how to start, you know? I mean we didn't know what was goin' on.

J. We was very young.

M. I was fourteen, she's twelve.

J. Daddy comes rushin' in one night, hollerin' 'Girls, girls, get up. We gotta go. We gotta go.' And he drags us outta bed, starts pullin' on our clothes –

M. There's all these bags in the hallway, all packed in a real hurry –

J. And we can hear some noise or sump'n –

M. Shoutin' and screamin'.

J. Momma's standin' there, watchin' the TV just – frozen, not movin' –

M. Daddy runnin' like a whirlin' dervish, grabbin' bags and –

J. And we see on the news there's a car on fire – a police car – and all these people round it – blacks and Hispanics – smashin' shop fronts and pullin' out TVs –

M. People throwin' bricks and and bottles and –

J. Police officers in helmets whuppin' six shades o' hell outta this black boy.

M. And then Daddy rushes over and yanks us up and starts pushin' us towards the door, toward the car.

J. Outside there's smoke comin' from downtown.

M. Orange glow from the fires.

J. We screamin' 'What's goin' on, Daddy?'

M. And he says 'It's the End o' the World – come just like I said it would.'

J. We got as far as the edge of Greenwood – where it cuts up on Main – and Daddy suddenly slams on the brake.

M. Road's blocked up ahead.

J. We gotta get out.

M. Do the rest on foot.

J. Daddy grabs all bags he can.

M. And he grabs our hands and he starts runnin' with us.

J. And then I says 'Where's Momma?'

M. We look back and she ain't movin'.

J. Daddy's yellin' her to come on.

M. But she's just standin' there terrified like – like she's turned to stone or sump'n.

J. And this man comes outta nowhere and he – he smacks her over the head – with a pipe – and she just – goes down. Crumbles like dust or sump'n.

M. And we's just frozen for a moment – like we don't know what to do.

J. And then I starts hollerin'.

M. We both do.

J. And we start runnin' towards her but Daddy stops us. Holds us back with his big hands and then he picks us up like we's as light as nightingales and he carries us off.

M. Through the fire and the smoke – glass crunchin' under his boots –

J. And we's howlin' 'Momma! Momma!' reachin' out for her lyin' there but he just keeps on goin', screamin' 'Don't look back, girls, don't look back.'

We managed to get outta the city that night. Inna diner the next mornin' out on the highway, watchin' it all on the TV. Whole city destroyed. Fires an' lootin'. Sheets coverin' up bodies lined up in the road.

M. One of 'em sheets coulda been our momma.

J. We says to Daddy, 'When we gonna go back home?'

M. But Daddy, says we ain't goin' back. He's done with ever'thin'.

J. They wanna rot in sin, they can have it.

M. Daddy kept us on the move. Kept us goin'. Kept us together.

J. He didn't trust no one else no more. Just us.

M. Said 'I don't need nothin' more in this world than you two girls. You ever'thin' to me.'

J. Now that Momma's gone, we's all the family he had left. And family's gotta stick together.

M. Amen.

J. Losin' Momma hit him real hard.

M. Though you'd never o' known at first.

J. Whenever we asked him he just say 'I didn't lose Momma – I see her ever'day. I can see her in your eyes and your smilin' faces.'

M. He put on a brave face for us. 'It's just you and me now, girls.'

J. The Three Musketeers.

M. We hit the road.

J. A big adventure.

M. Travelled far as we could, motel to motel.

J. I liked that part. Every day a clean new room. Spotless.

M. Spick and span.

J. We kept ourselves to ourselves, mostly.

M. Daddy'd get real mean round people.

J. I mean, Daddy's always been a passionate man –

M. Sure, anyone could see that.

J. Course – and he'd never been angry, but there was times with us when he's just more –

M. He started gettin' in these awful black moods in the car drivin'. Hundred miles down the road, wouldn't say a single word. Just stare on out at the road ahead.

J. You didn't wanna say nothin' in case –

M. And then all o' sudden he'd turn round right as rain again.

J. You couldn't tell one minute to the next what he's gonna be like.

M. Some days he'd be Good Daddy, and when he's like that you couldn't ask for a kinder, more lovin' father. And then other days he – he –

J. Well, he just wasn't.

M. He started drinkin'. I mean, he drank before though he's always a moderate man.

J. But now you'd see him on the porch o' the motel, swiggin' on a beer, just starin' out on the world, givin' it the evil eye like he's lookin' for sump'n to start trouble.

M. And we'd come over and be like 'What you lookin' at, Daddy?'

J. And he's say 'Nothin'. Get inside now, girls. I mean it. Get inside now, get.'

M. He was gettin' mean like that ever' day now.

J. We stopped drivin'. Came to fix in a place I don't know where.

M. Didn't like us goin' outside none.

J. Like he's guardin' us, almost jealous like.

M. And then one day he stopped lettin' us leave the motel room at all.

J. I went out to get some ice for my soda, an' I open the door and all o' sudden he's like 'Where you goin'?' And I says 'I'm gonna get some ice, Daddy.' And he says 'No you ain't. You come back here now.' And I say 'I'll only be a moment, Daddy, I promise –' and 'fore I can finish what I'm sayin' he comes over and slams the door like that.

M. Near came off its hinges.

J. Caught my finger in the jamb.

M. That near came off too.

J. It near did. I started hollerin' and screamin', blood gushin' out – and Daddy realises what he gone done and like that he just switches –

M. Just changes.

J. Starts apologisin', tellin' me he never meant to hurt his baby girl. I still got the scar to prove it – there. Just there, see?

M. Ain't the only one she got. Me neither. See that? That's a belt buckle. And that's a beer bottle.

J. We ain't left that room in days.

M. Weeks. Hell, it coulda been months, years, I don't know.

J. The place is startin' to stink now. We ain't gettin' any fresh air in there.

M. Daddy won't open the windows. Won't even let us open the curtains. Piles of ol' takeout layin' all over the place.

J. He'd look at us and be like 'What you girls lookin at? Lookin', lookin', y'always lookin' at me like – Just get, alright? Get! You's getting on my nerves!'

M. Spend the whole time walkin' round like we's on broken glass.

J. Only peace we'd get's when he'd go out into town.

M. Probably go sit in a bar and stew for a while.

J. And even then we wouldn't leave or nothin'. We's just glad to get some peace from it. We's so scared we didn't even dare peel back the curtains to look out at the stars.

M. Then one night we's lyin' in bed, wrapped up in each other like little S's, tryna sleep. Daddy been out a good while and the room is nice and quiet and calm. Then all a sudden we hear a scratchin' at the lock.

J. He can't get in – he's so drunk he can't get in.

M. And then he starts thumpin' on the door. Starts thumpin' and hollerin' 'Girls! Girls! Girls, open up!'

J. And neither one of us moves. We hopin' like if we don't say nothin', maybe he'll go away.

M. He starts screamin' 'Open up! Open up, you miserable little – ' and then he starts kickin' the door. Kicks it and kicks it and it bursts in off its hinges and he comes bowlin' in drunk as all hell –

J. And he comes over and he yells 'What the hell you playin' at? Didn't you hear me?' and I's like 'We's asleep, Daddy' and he yells 'Don't lie to me!' and he drags me offa the bed and starts hittin' me and hittin' me and –

M. And I's like 'Stop it, Daddy, stop, please stop!' and all a sudden he turns round and screams 'Don't look at me! Don't you fuckin' look at me! You always lookin' at me like her, like – like – Why you gotta look at me like her?'

And he starts – he starts cryin'. Snot dribblin' down his chin. Head in his hands, shoulders shakin', he looks – so small. And I puts my hand out on his shoulders and I say 'It's okay, it's okay.'

And he's cryin' and mumblin' I don't know what when he reaches out and he takes my hand and he squeezes it tight against his face. And he calls me by my momma's name.

And he starts kissin' my hand. Starts holdin' and kissin' it, layin' his head deep into my chest and starts sobbin'. And I'm goin' 'It's okay, it's okay.'

J. 'I missed you', he says.

M. 'I missed you too', I says.

J. 'I never meant to leave you. I'm sorry.'

M. 'I know.'

J. 'I'm so – '

M. 'Shh shh, s'alright. We alright, baby, we alright.' And he holds me closer, tight as he possibly can, and he reaches up and he kisses me. He kisses me again. I try to push him off but he's bigger, and I – I just lay there and I – I let him – wait for him to –

And his whole body goes stiff and quivers and he's done. Flops down on toppa me. Sweat drippin' offa him. And he lifts himself up and he looks down at me. And for a split second there's absolute peace in his face. And I say 'It's okay. It's okay, Daddy.'

And sump'n switches in his eye. And I look up at him again. I look him in the eye. And all that peace he had just before just – crumbles. Like dust.

And then he jolts all a sudden. Jolts real quick and then stops. And then a little trickle of blood runs down from his head, and he looks at it like 'Whose blood is that?' Then his eyes roll back and he flops like a fish. And my sister's standin' there with a cracked lamp in her hand. Her face all battered and bust up. Cracked like the lamp. Nose flat, eye purple, blood all o'er her cheek. And she's smilin' too.

She ain't smiled in ages.

J. We buried him under a tree by a brook. He woulda liked it there. It was quiet and there weren't no people. When we layed him down he looked just like the Daddy we remembered. Real peaceful, like. Handsome and dignified. Like he's finally gonna have the rest he deserves. We's proud we could give him that.

M. We didn't leave a name or nothin' tellin' people he was there.

J. Weren't nobody else's business.

M. People didn't need to know. Just us. That was all's important. Name's just a name, you know?

J. Took time for us to get used to ours. The new ones, I mean. Doctors and the Social Services kept usin' them, but it took forever for 'em to stick. They'd call us by our new names and we'd jus' be standin' there starin' into space not knowin' they's talkin' to us.

M. That's kids for you, though. Always a million miles away in their own little worlds. Like my little one there. Billy! Billy! See – still can't hear nothin', even with the window – Too busy horsin' about with his dad.

J. Chuck's real good with him.

M. Oh, so good. And he was never funny 'bout it. I mean, people sometimes say sump'n. Look at me and say I ain't old enough to be his mother.

J. Ain't people's business. That's ours. Ain't between nobody 'cept us. We's family. And family's the most important thing you got.

M. Amen to that.

J. Amen.

The Thief on the Cross

A prison cell on Death Row.

THE THIEF *sits on the edge of his bunk in a prison issue jumpsuit.*

THE THIEF. Ain't nobody tryna make a film 'bout me.

Tha's the third time that faggoty-ass German's been in here wid them cameras. You can't see him 'less you squeeze yo'self right up 'gainst the corner of the cell, push your face 'gainst the glass. Him and his camera guy, two guards standin' either side of 'em, and they's talkin' wid him all nice and polite like they's havin' a normal conversation or sump'n.

'How zey treating you? Do you haff anyzing to say to your supporters?'

His voice, his accent, man, sounds so faggoty. You can't hardly unnerstan' what he's sayin', I wanna be like 'Speak English, motherfucker!' And then when you hear him talk back it's like – man, it's like –

S'like living next door to a fuckin' celebrity. Motherfucker gets more mail than Santa. I only ever seen him the one time. When they bringin' him back to his cell one time. Pale-lookin' motherfucker, real skinny but you look at his eyes and they are like – blue, I mean real fuckin' blue, like sky or sump'n. And this fuckin' grin on his lips like –

He gets 'em from all sorts – the letters, I mean. I hear him read them out in that voice, man. He reads 'em out. People sayin' they believe in him. Tellin' him not to give up hope, they prayin' for his release ever' day. Newspapers askin' for exclusives on him. Women declarin' their undyin' love for him. He always got a little smile in his voice when he reads them ones – like he find it sweet or funny or sump'n, like they don't know better. All these women so eager to please him they breakin' their hips tryna get their legs open quick enough.

I useta tell him to shut up, useta yell 'cross at him 'You keep goin' on like that an' I'm gonna come on in there and break my foot off in yo' ass!' but that just make him read mo'. Guy on the other side can't get enough of it. He's like 'Oh read one to me, won't you, read one for me please.' And first I think he's jus' jackin' off to all the dirty ones but then I realise that he's listenin' to them like a little kid bein' read a bedtime story or sump'n. Fallin' for him hook, line and sinker.

Says he believes in him. Oh yeah. Yeah, man, I hear him one night, after lights out, through the wall, jus' talkin' talkin' talkin' and him next door listenin' patiently 'Mmm-hmm' and then the other guy's cryin' beggin' him to save him an' all that shit. And this motherfucker says

'You are forgiven. Bless you, my child'

and the other guy's so fuckin' happy he's like cryin' and laughin' like a fuckin' baby.

Boy started losin' his mind, man. S'what happens when they stick you in box five years. Changes you, you ain't normal no mo'. You start forgettin' the world's bigger than ten by six. You start thinkin' small and then your mind gets small, know what I'm sayin'? Like – Like I's lyin' on my bunk th'other night and I's lookin' at my toe. My big toe. I's lookin' at it and thinkin' all about it. How it got here. Like – like we useta all be like fish or sump'n with like little fins and then one day we's like monkeys swinging around in the trees and shit and I just can't figure how we got from that to that, know what I'm sayin? And then I start thinkin' 'bout it like it's jus' a big finger that can't do nothin'. And then I'm like 'What the fuck am I doin' thinkin' 'bout my motherfuckin' toe for?' I ain't never done shit like that on the outside. But then you start thinkin' 'bout other shit – like – like yo' wrists and yo' hands and then that ain't enough. You start looking deeper. At your blood and your bones. Pokin' round in the shit you find in there. Shit you ain't thought 'bout in years. Start goin' deeper an' deeper, and 'fore you know it you find yo'self down at the bottom. And it's cold and dark down there. Pressure's comin' down on you, crushin' your lungs and you can't breathe no more and you can't move your arms, and you try to scream and but nothin'

comin' out and you think you gonna die and you start
screamin' and screamin' and then you realise you ain't
nowhere. You right back in here where you was before.

Makes you small, man, makes you small in here. And that's
when he tries to get you. When you at your weakest.

He starts talkin' to me through the wall.

'Hey – you okay? I thought I heard you cryin'.'

And I don't say nothin'.

'I don't sleep much neither,'

he says.

'Always do my best thinkin' at night, when it's quiet. Jus'
you and the big wide world and nothin' else but the peace
and quiet.'

'I ain't gettin' no peace and quiet wid you around,'

I says.

'I knew you were awake,'

he says and I can tell he's smilin' as he says it. Like he gone
tricked me or sump'n. And he asks me wassup and I'm like

'What's it to you?'

And he says he just wants to know. As a brother.

'You ain't no brother o' mine.'

'We all brothers,'

he says,

'don't matter what we look like. Tha's what I always tell
people.'

'That what got you in here?'

'Lotta things brought me here,'

he says,

'but in a way, yes.' Says he weren't too popular on the
outside and tha's why they put him in here.

I ax him,

'Well, if you ain't so popular how come's you keep gettin' so much fan mail? How come you getting 'portant visitors and people makin' movies about you?'

He says there's lots of people that do like him, sure, but some people – 'portant people, people in power – they weren't too partial to it so they made sure he wind up in here.

'You mus' be pretty mad at them folks who stitched you up then.'

No, no he ain't mad. Says he forgives 'em cos they don't know what they doin'.

'Ain't that mighty generous of you.'

And then I says,

'Way I figger it, though, ever'body got a reason for bein' in here. Like your friend over there, on the other side. He ain't in here on the Row for jaywalkin'. He in here cos he gone done burnt down a school wid two little kids inside.'

And he says

'So, why are you in here then?'

That stumped me, that did.

I been here five year. Five years. I useta be out in the Projects. Grew up there. Raisin' hell and my momma's blood pressure. I get in all kindsa trouble with my cousin, been in and outta juvenile once or twice but nothin' big. After the second time I got my girl knocked up and I figger 'Shit I'm gonna be a daddy. I better start gettin' 'sponsible.' And I did. Got a job, locksmith – good wid my hands – and I stopped rollin' wid my boys, my cousin, started actin' real good, keepin' onna straight and narrow. Then one day this little ol' lady accuses me o' stealin'. She a mean ol' lady, mean as catshit. I changed her locks for her and two weeks later she gets broken in to. Accuses me of copyin' the keys, which is bullshit, so – So I get questioned, my file gets pulled up. And it's all bullshit, they didn't charge me or nothin' but work don't like it so they let me go. Leave me wid a wife and a baby and no way to put food onna table. Fuck am I gonna do now?

Then one day my cousin calls. I ain't heard from the boy in time, but says he wants to meet me. Got a favour wants to ax me. I says sure but I ain't got no car no mo' – they took the van wit' the fuckin' – but he says don't worry 'bout it, he gonna come by my place pick me up.

Hour later, I'm cruising through my ol' stompin' grounds wit' mah cousin. Seein' all the ol' places we useta go when we was lil kids, all the places we useta hang. They all look so much smaller than they useta be, but then again ever'thin' look big when you three-foot-nothin'. I see the ol' faces out there, all the usual crew, talkin', hollerin' 'Where you been at, boy?' an' it's kinda nice, you know, it's kinda – Like goin' down Memory Lane or sump'n but – And we sittin' outside my cousin's crib, out in the yard, smokin', drinkin'. He's sparkin' up and I don't do that no mo', but I ain't gonna say no to sharin' a forty on a sunny fuckin' day, know what I'm sayin'?

And my cousin, man, he askin' me how it goin' on the straight an' narrow and normally, man, I'd be like, yeah it's all good, man, it's all – But I ain't feelin' that today, truth be told, I ain't feelin' – So I tell him the truth, you know? Lay it out like – like what I'm fuckin' feelin' and not havin' no job or nothin' or not knowin' what the fuck I'm gonna do, man, what I'm gonna fuckin' –

And my cuz, man, he looks at me real quiet like, like he's listenin', man, noddin' listenin', 'fore he blows out this big stream o' smoke up in the air and says,

'I got a job for you, man.'

'A job?'

I say,

'What kinda job?'

'Good one,'

he says,

'Pay well. Need me a locksmith and a lookout. Someone who's good. Someone I can trust. You interested?'

Interested? Sure I'm interested. I'm fuckin' des'p'rate. He smiles at me and says 'A'it', meet him at the corner of

Fairfax and Sullivan tonight at midnight, boys'll pick me up then. I says 'A'it' and we done. We walk on over back to his car and takes me home, tells me again: 'Midnight, corner of Fairfax and Sullivan, don't be late.'

Tell my wife I'm goin' out that night. Friend got a friend who might have a job, wants him to meet me. Have a drink wit' him or sump'n cos he's real casual like, he ain't into all that kinda, you know, like, meetin' interview bullshit and that, but it might be sump'n, you know, so I gotta go. I tell her not to wait up, I won't wake her when I come back, and I go in our bedroom where my lil baby girl's sleepin' in a crib in the corner. Look down at her and her lil chest risin' an' fallin', risin' an' fallin', like lil waves, you know – and I kiss her on the forehead 'fore I grab my coat and my kit and I head outta the door.

Midnight, my cousin pulls up, I get in the back o' his ride with his boys and we drive on up to this old place out on Maple, up inna Hills. Twenty minutes later, I'm on my knees picking my way through a Yale lock and normally I'd be, like, in there in like two minutes flat, like, but it's a lil fuckin' bit harder when you got four boys hangin' over you watching what you doin' and you ain't tryna be noticed by no fucker who might jus' be walkin' by at any minute, you know? My hands are, like, shakin' an' sweatin' but I manage to pop the lock an' inna minute we inside, my cousin and the others leadin' the way, 'fore turns to me an' says

'You on point,'

and he hands me a .45. Ain't held one in a time. Feels like a weight in my hand.

I stand waitin' out there for what feels like fo' fuckin' ever, peepin' out the window an' shit case I see anybody suspicious or nothin'. I ain't movin', ain't fuckin' breathin', keepin' still as I can, like, but someone mussa heard us cos it ain't long 'fore we see blue lights pullin' up out front. I start panickin', man, an' I run down the hall to tell my cousin but he mussa heard 'em too cos 'fore I even get there they be comin' down the stairs like fuckin' lightnin' headin' fo' the back door. They don't even stop fo' me, holla out fo' me to come follow but I don't need askin', I's already runnin' after

them, out through the back door, inna the yard, heart beatin'
like a fuckin' engine, lungs burstin' and burnin' – shit, man,
I outta shape, I got fat all that time sittin' on my ass
locksmithin' – runnin' after them over the grass, watchin'
them take the fence in one go and inna second I's there with
them, over the fence and landin' on the other side like a
fuckin' sack o' shit but 'fore I can run I hear this 'Don't
move!' screamin' at me and turn round and without thinkin'
– without thinkin' 'bout the .45 in my hand – I turn round
and pull the trigger.

He's only a kid, man. Twenty-three, tops. Baby-soft skin and
a face that looked like he didn't know what the fuck was
goin' on when he fell. And I didn't mean to do it, I didn't
mean – I's just reactin, like, I's just doin' it without thinkin'
but like – like – I mean – I mean, what's a fuckin' kid like
that doin' in uniform?

I's the only one caught. 'S all on me. Judge was smiling
when he sent me down and I been here ever since. Five years
and waitin' for the chair.

'I forgive you,' he says.

What?

'I forgive you,' he says, and I can hear that smile in his
voice, like he so fuckin' patient and unnerstandin', 'I forgive
you, and He will too. In the hereafter.'

Fuck you, man.

'Believe me and believe in me and He will forgive you in the
hereafter – '

You think I give a good goddamn about your forgiveness in
the hereafter? You think that gonna stop them puttin' a crown
on my head and forty thousand volts through my body?

'He will forgive you – '

What use his forgiveness gonna be when I'm six feet
unnergroun'? What fuckin' use is that to me? Where is it
now? Where's my forgiveness now?

'If you want to be forgiven, you have to be sorry – '

You think I ain't sorry 'bout what I done? You think I ain't – Ain't a day go by when I don't think 'bout that boy and what I taken from him, ain't a day go by that I don't – And I ain't sorry just cos I end up in here, man, I ain't – I am sorry, I'm well and truly sorry, but – but – What good's killin' me gonna do? What good's fuckin' – That gonna bring him back? That gonna bring him back from the fuckin' – They wanna take my life, they take it, man, they already took it, they already fuckin' – They lock me up in here, put me in a fuckin' box, taken ever'thin' I loved, ever'thin' I ever – Leave me to – I ain't got no more to give, man, I ain't – I paid for what I done, I paid for it in here but that ain't enough, man, that ain't – They wanna take my life from me, they wanna take my – But it ain't theirs to take, man, it ain't theirs to – Just like it weren't mine to take that boy's life, it ain't theirs to take mine, man, so why are they like – Why's it alright for them to – I mean, how is that fair, man? How is that fuckin' fair?

And he says,

'My father moves in mysterious ways,'

and I say 'You think I care? Who the fuck I care? My daddy wasn't nobody, you think I care you the son o' God?'

'Everything has a purpose.'

Fuck you say?

'Everything has a – '

Fuck your purpose. What was His purpose when he took my job, huh? When He made my baby girl starve? When He put that gun in my hand? What was his purpose then? I asked for forgiveness from them, I said I'm sorry, I went down on my knees and wept but they didn't wanna hear none of it. And now He got me in here, that motherfucker gonna ask me to crawl over to him on my hands and knees and beg for His forgiveness? He outta his goddamn motherfuckin' mind.

'I'm sorry,' he said.

Don't be fuckin' sorry.

'I'm sorry you cannot believe in me. Cannot believe in Him.'

On no, you wrong about that, boy. You wrong about that.
You din't ax me to believe in Him. You asked me to beg Him
for forgiveness. But you don't have to ax me to believe in
Him. I seen Him. I seen His work and His mysterious ways.
I seen him put motherfuckers like me down in the middle of
the motherfuckin' earth, pushin' and proddin' me around,
throwin' shit at me, knockin' me down every goddamn time
I get cocky enough to think I can stand up proud on my own
to two feet fo' a change till he got me here lyin' and bleedin'
on the fuckin' floor and then He asks me to kiss his boots and
say 'thank you'?

Way I see it, that motherfucker oughta drag His sorry ass
down offa His high-and-mighty throne, come down here and
get down on His fucking knees and beg me for my
forgiveness. Cos I sure as hell ain't doin' it for Him.

Songbook Appendix

Keep On Smilin'

Sure as sunshine leads to rain
Sure as true love leads to pain
This old life of yours is tryna wear you down
But there is a simple way
You can brighten up your day
Lose those worries, lose those sorrows, lose that frown

And just keep smilin', smilin' no matter what you do
Keep on smilin', smilin' and it'll get you through
As we walk through life trudging mile after mile
Things will look that much better if you smile

When your landlord wants the rent
And your money's all been spent
On some lowlife who left you up the creek
Don't be sad, don't be blue
I'll tell you what to do
To find the happiness you seek

You just keep smilin', smilin' no matter what you do
Keep on smilin', smilin' and it'll get you through
As we walk through life trudging mile after mile
Things will look that much better if you smile

Well you may have hit the bottom
Of the bottle cos you got them
Problems stacked high into the sky
But you can bet your bottom nickel
That through all the thin and thick I'll
Be smiling right beside you by your side

So just keep smilin', smilin' no matter what you do
Keep on smilin', smilin' and it'll get you through

As we walk through life trudging mile after mile
Things will look that much better if you smile

And just keep smilin', smilin' no matter what you do
Keep on smilin', smilin' and it'll get you through
As we walk through life trudging mile after mile
Things will look that much better if you smile

12 Prison Bar Blues

Woke up this morning
Locked up inside a prison cell
Woke up this morning
Locked up inside a prison cell
Looked at those prison bars
I thought I'd died and gone to hell

My little darlin'
She's waitin' for me outside
My little darlin'
She's waitin' for me outside
When she found out I's in here
Lord, you shoulda heard how she cried

I ain't a bad man
But I gone done a bad, bad thing
I ain't a bad man
But I gone done a bad, bad thing
And come tomorrow
The judge man says I'm gonna swing

I shot a young man
His skin turned pale as he turned dead
I shot a young man
His skin turned pale as he turned dead
My skin is black, my heart is blue
And both my hands is stained blood red

I ain't afraid to die
To wear that noose and kick this world
I ain't afraid to die
To wear that noose and kick this world
But there's just one thing that scares me:
Who gonna feed my baby girl?

(Cos The Man I Love, My Darlin') He Don't Treat Me Right

I can't sleep a wink, my dearest
I can't sleep at night
Cos the man I love, my darlin'
He don't treat me right

I can't stomach food, my honey
I can't eat a bite
Cos the man I love, my darlin'
He don't treat me right

Can't see colours any more
I try but it's no use
Purples, greens and reds are gone
All that's left is black and blue

I can't stand the daytime, precious
I can't stand the light
Cos the man I love, my darlin'
He don't treat me right
Cos the man I love, my darlin'
He don't treat me right

Oh Death

O Death, O Death
Just look what you gone done done
O Death, O Death
Just look what you gone done done
O Death, O Death
Just look what you gone done done
You took my woman and left me alone

It was two in the morning
When Death walked in the room
It was two in the morning
When Death walked in the room
It was two in the morning
When Death walked in the room
Took my woman, left my bed like a tomb

You stole my woman
And took her to the other side
You stole my woman
And took her to the other side
You stole my woman
And took her to the other side
When I saw she'd gone, Lord how I cried

O Death, don't leave me
Alone on Earth so cold
O Death, don't leave me
Alone on Earth so cold
O Death, don't leave me
Alone on Earth so cold
I don't wanna be alone and old

O when will Death
Come take me from this woe
O when will Death
Come take me from this woe
O when will Death
Come take me from this woe
Lord don't keep me here, I'm ready to go

'I Went Down to Galilee'

I went down, I went down
I went down to Galilee
I went down, I went down
To see exactly what I could see
What did I see, what did I see
What did I see in Galilee?
I saw the Lord
And he's waiting there for me

Galilee! Galilee!

I heard him preach, I heard him preach
I heard him preach at Galilee
The words so sweet, the words so sweet
The words so sweet just like honey
What did he say, what did he say
What did he say at Galilee?
He said 'Rejoice!
And your spirit will be free!'

Galilee! Galilee!

I saw the wounds, I saw the wounds
Upon his hands and in his side
The wounds so deep, the wounds so deep
The wounds so deep he shoulda died
But he arose, but he arose
And came before us where he cried
'I am the Lord!
Your saviour and your guide!'

Galilee! Galilee!

He took me to, He took me to
The River Jordan, clean and blue
He washed my sins, he washed my sins
He cleaned my soul as good as new
He did it for me, He did it for me
And he can sure do it for you
Just say 'Amen!'
And he'll come to your rescue.

Galilee! Galilee!
Galilee! Galilee!

SAVE + QUIT

Sophia Leuner

This version of *Save + Quit* was first performed at VAULT Festival, London, on 8 February 2017, with the following cast:

JOE	Eddie Joe Robinson
STEPH	Josie Charles
CARA	Niamh Branigan
DYLAN	Peter Mooney
Directors	Billie de Buitléar
	Sophia Leuner

With special thanks to my trusty editor Billie, my friends Karan and Caoimhe, the very large de Buitléar family, and the very small Chetin-Leuner family.

Characters

PART ONE, LONDON
JOE, *male, twenties, London*
STEPH, *female, twenties, Hull*

PART TWO, DUBLIN
CARA, *female, twenties, Tallaght*
DYLAN, *male, twenties, Dalkey*

Note on Play

This play is to be performed on a bare stage, with no or limited set or props.

The play is divided into monologues. Within these, the characters fully embody the different people they encounter or recall.

The characters can be lit simultaneously or separately.

A forward slash (/) marks the point of interruption in overlapping dialogue.

PART ONE

JOE. I was supposed to be meeting this girl in Regent's Park
    so we could go on a walk or something, I dunno, but when
    the Bakerloo line pulled in I didn't want to get off – we'd
    only been out a few times – so I stayed on, thought I'd go
    visit my mum instead. I got off ten stops and half an hour
    later at Willesden Junction. Tapped out and ran into someone
    I knew –

'Oi my man! Long time no see.'

We went to school together. I didn't like him much –

'What brings you back, man?'

'You know, visiting my mum.'

'Fair fair. Oi you know, you should come out wiv us later
    we're going to – '

'Cheers bruv, but I gotta run, nice catching up, man, hope
    you're good.'

He thought I was being rude and I guess I was but I couldn't
    be bothered, you know? I hate coming back here because
    you run into all these people you thought you were never
    gonna see again. The corner shops are run by the same
    people and the same shit is being repaired. This ain't
    London. It's grey and shit and flat. But it's actually what
    most of London is. Places like this.

STEPH. My interview was really weird. I went in and the
    headteacher, this *munter* with wrinkly cleavage shook my
    hand. She smelt like new car and stale cigarettes. Before
    I even sat down she was like

'What did you study at Birmingham then?'

'Geography,' I say, and I want to seem friendly, you know, so
    I add – 'my family always say I chose Birmingham because
    it was a few miles closer to London.'

It isn't well received.

'You have good scores on ITIT and great references, why do you want to work here?'

It wasn't asked like you would expect a job interview to go, you know? It was all like passive aggressive. I ignored it though.

'In my opinion, a teacher should help those who are less advantaged than his or herself. Eastbury Comprehensive is a place where I can give back to the community and educate those who are just as worthy of an education as the rest of the country, and yet are often neglected – '

'Okay. You're one of those. Fine. Twenty-one starting salary, if you last a year, it will go up.'

JOE. My mum hobbled round the kitchen fixing me something to eat.

(*Middle-aged, with any accent indicating she is a first-generation immigrant.*) 'Look I need to tell you something. I don't want you to shout. I don't want you to get angry. But... I'm... I'm moving.'

I couldn't believe it. Mum had lived here for, like, thirty years.

'This house is too big for me, I'm moving to your aunt's – '

'In Wembley? Why it's a shithol– '

'Don't you swear at me, young man. You have your own flat now, you never come round here. With my hip the stairs are hard and – '

She kept going, listing loads of good reasons why she should move. Closer to family. Memory of Dad. Dangerous. House prices in London. It all made sense.

'You take the Xbox with you today.'

STEPH. 'No it's an X, she's done a tick, they are very anal – I mean fussy – about this stuff. Could you please tell her that? Could you tell her now please? Kabita? Could you translate that for your mum please? Kabita, this is important. She has ticked in the box but she needs to start again and put an X instead.'

It was six thirty on a Tuesday evening and I had been at one of my student's homes for the past two hours.

'You said anal!'

There were six kids running about and their mother was sitting next to me looking at me with this desperate look like...

'You need to start again,' I say. But she just blinked at me.

'Kabita... I'll come back tomorrow with a new form.'

JOE. My dad bought me an Xbox for my eighth birthday. It was one of those gifts which is just as much for the person buying the present as it is for the person they're giving it to. We played together a lot, almost every day. He'd come home from work and I'd be like – 'Let's play let's play' and he'd be like

'One sec let me get changed and see your mum. Hello sweetheart' – he'd kiss 'er.

'Dad Dad Dad Dad Dad Dad.'

'Yeah, alright I'm coming. What game is it tonight then?'.

Our favourite was this racing game – 'RALLY SPORTS CHALLENGE.' He was so good at it. I loved that he never let me win. Mum would be like 'Let him win he's only young' and Dad would look at her and say 'Exactly. He's young, he's winning at everything else. Let me win this time.'

And I'd always lose. I don't remember a time when I beat him, and you would have thought he'd have let me win at least once. We played so much. And when I started school, I'd still make time to play with him.

When he died I couldn't touch it for ages, maybe six years, I dunno. But one day I thought fuck it and started playing our game.

So I sat down and opened it and I forgot that you have this thing called the ghost driver. It's a setting where when you race, the fastest lap gets recorded and you play against it to improve, you know it? So cos my dad was so good, all his races were saved. Now this little blob of a car – all see-through and like floating – was my dad.

I played and played till I got good enough to beat him but
I paused the game right in front of the finish line so I wouldn't
delete my dad's score. I go back on it sometimes but I keep
pausing it in that second before…

I haven't moved it to my place in Catford (I know, I literally
moved from one shithole to another) but I guess today
I have to.

STEPH. It's an easy commute, I guess. Well, people tell me it is.
I live in the Turnpike Lane-ish area so I get the Victoria line
two stops to *Blackhorse Road* (great name, I know right) I still
get excited by some of the stop names, like *Mansion House*
and *Island Gardens* and – (*Singing the song.*) *Warwick
Avenue*… Anyway I change at Blackhorse Road and get the
Overground – the ginger one – to Barking. It takes me about
forty-five minutes. The first couple of weeks were terrifying.
I always wanted to cry because I was so tired all the time and
I had this stupid idea in my head that I could do all my
marking on the commute. Like sit with all the books and tick
tick cross sticker sticker smiley-face. But there are no seats.
EVER. And people are so rude 'Excuse me' or 'Do you
mind?' and then it's always like on the day you are covering
registration for the head of your department that you happen to
get the train which – 'will be held here to even out gaps in the
service'. And I stand there squashed in this sweat gland and I
just want to scream STOP STEPPING ON MY FEET AND
LET ME SIT DOWN YOU BLOODY DICKHEADS – I'VE
BEEN ON MY FEET ALL DAY AND BEEN YELLED AT
FOR NINE HOURS STRAIGHT BY A LOAD OF TINY
LITTLE SHITS – OH AND YOU, MADAM, WITH YOUR
WHOLE FOODS PRODUCE, CLEARLY NEED TO REST
YOUR WEARY LEGS FROM A LONG DAY OF
SHOPPING FOR ORGANIC VEGETABLES…

I obviously never do though.

JOE. I carried the Xbox back home on the Tube in its original
box that my mum had kept. Of course she kept the fucking
box. I left it in the kitchen then went on a walk. I never go
on walks what the fuck? I walked for ages. Then I got on
a train and went back to where me and my ex used to live.
I remember the estate agent taking us round the flat –

'And this carpet, just look at it, I could eat it. And I'm almost forgetting the best bit – there's a view of Westfield from your bathroom window.'

Oh great! I remember thinking, everyone's dream: to be reminded you're broke while taking a shit.

The light switched on in the bathroom and I realised how fucking nuts I must look, staring at my old flat. I left and saw the homeless guy who always sits outside the station, saw some underage kids drinking on the green, saw the line for that shitty club which used to be public toilets, saw the building where I used to work, with some of the office lights still on...

STEPH. I woke up early to get Kabita's mum a new form. I printed it off at school cos it was forty pages long. But just as I was finishing, Simon came in to the staffroom.

'What are you doing in so early?'

Simon teaches PE. A subject he believes to be far superior to all others.

'What you got there?'

'A housing benefit form for Kabita's family.'

I tried to leave but he lunged and blocked my exit, then felt bad about it so awkwardly moved out of my way.

'Hey. Why don't you come to the pub tonight? It's Mark's birthday.'

'I don't know Mark.'

'You know *me*.'

...Ah.

JOE. I woke up late and put the Xbox online to sell. Low price. Games included. The box was still sitting there though so I wanted to get out the flat. I didn't know what to do. I looked through my phone to see if there was anyone I felt like calling. There wasn't. I went to The Ritzy cos they were showing *Annie Hall*. I like the opening of that film. He's like:

He tries to imitate Woody Allen's Groucho Marx joke from the opening monologue of Annie Hall.

Sounds about right to me.

STEPH. 'I need to help Kabita first.' I said, still trying to scoot around Simon.

'You need to have fun too.'

'Yeah, well, maybe I'll pop by after. See you.'

'Wait, you don't even know what pub we'll be at.'

'I'll text you.'

'You don't have my number.'

'I'll – '

'Hey! You can't keep ignoring everyone. You've barely spoken to anyone since starting here, you disappear the minute the bell rings...'

JOE. There was still no sign of interest on the Xbox. I applied for some jobs before going to my shift. My line manager greets me at the door:

'Tinder Tuesdays! Ready to get busy?'

Fuck off! – I thought. At least I get good tips cos the guys want to look all generous in front of their dates. But it is weird how everyone seems to have the same idea and all say 'Tuesday sound good? I know this cute pub we can go to.'

It's one of those things – those things where the coincidence is like too simple or convenient – so you think that the world must exist inside your head, you get me? Like everyone is just a figment of your imagination that you create because they're a part of your –

'Excuse me.'

'Sorry, mate,' I say, snapping back into reality. Or *my* reality... Who knows! 'What can I get you?'

'Yeah – a San Miguel and – What was it again? Yeah, a Pinot Grigio I think is what she said.'

'Small or large?'

'Large. Yeah large, definitely.' (*Winks*.)

STEPH. I come from a big family but my home was never as noisy as this one.

'Kabita, where's your dad?'

'He's not here yet'

But at that moment one of the kids tripped over the baby and both started screaming. The mum jumped up and stopped the crying in less than a minute. I was impressed. She was firm-handed yet very adoring at the same time. The other kids got jealous with the attention the two were getting and started kicking up a fuss. Knocking wooden spoons about, I was so jumpy, all those pointed edges and sharp things. At school if there's an arts-and-crafts lesson where we need to get the scissors out I have to drink a bottle of wine when I get home just to get my stress level down.

I thought what my brothers would be doing now – probably playing on their games-console thing. My mum would leave them there knowing that no harm would come to them – physical anyway. I was always taught video games turn kids' brains to mush but they like it and it keeps them quiet and calm so who gives a shit.

There was this loud knocking on the wall and the kids fell silent like that. One of the younger ones ran under her mother's dress.

Knock.

Again.

'SHUT THE FUCK UP YOU FUCKING PAKIS.'

Pause.

'Kabita… Does this happen a lot?'

She nods.

'Is it your next-door neighbours?'

She nods again.

I go to open the door but Kabita's mum grabs hold of my elbow and shakes her head.

'It's not – 'She smiled at me as if to say 'I know it's not fair.'

'You're not even Pakistani' I say as she gives me a folder full of papers. They basically gave all the documentation that she needs to apply for larger benefits. There were receipts for bills that had all been paid on time but there were easily four rejection letters from the council denying her any more money. There were three notices for outstanding bedroom tax. I didn't understand it completely or as well I as I should but something was clearly wrong and there were huge gaps where she should be supported. I counted the rooms but there weren't any spare –

'Mama was pregnant when we came to London,' Kabita said, looking over my shoulder at the forms.

I stared at her.

'Can you understand this, Kabita?'

Kabita shrugs her shoulders as if to say 'it's no big deal'.

'Well done.' I said, amazed.

This eleven-year-old was incredible. She spoke flawless English, scored better than most of her classmates on pretty much everything, and on top of that, understood that her family was being ripped off. For the first time since moving to London, I felt genuine affection for someone.

I carefully filled out the form, doing an 'X' in the boxes and I attached a letter in my best handwriting explaining the pregnancy, giving them no excuse to be racist shits.

'Thanks. I'm teaching my mama English but she is slow.'

I put a first-class stamp on it and sent it off. Then I got the bus home.

JOE (*Steph's headteacher*). 'Is there a minimum card spend?'

It's eleven thirty. Last orders. The queue is easily five people deep. This woman has ordered at least three rounds and paid with card every single time and yet she still needs to ask if there's a minimum card spend?

'Yeah. Ten pounds.'

She's gross. Make-up all sweaty, pinky lipstick on her teeth, wrinkled. Her bra's too tight and it's making her skin pop out around the straps by her armpits. She smells like wet fags and... car freshener?

'Shit... Really?'

No. I'm joking.

''Fraid so yeah.'

'Well, I guess I'll have three Southern Comfort and – '

' – and lemonade. Yeah. Coming right up.'

It's then that I see her. My ex-girlfriend with that cunt who ordered the large – (*Winks*.) Pinot Grigio. She's staring at me from the back of the queue. She does this cute little nervous wave. And I do this awkward polite nod. I try and focus on doing the rest of the queue but I'm all self-conscious and like, I know she's looking at me and I dunno whether to suck in my belly or flip a bottle or something but while I'm thinking about that I forget my orders and drop the money I'm holding cos my hands have gotten all sweaty and my line manager is all like 'Come on almost there keep it up!'

STEPH. I really want to help these children. I don't know why and I don't think I need to ask why, I'm helping them because they need to be helped. My mum took me to see this play with Bill Nighy in it – that's why she took me – 'Bill Nighy and that girl from *The Great Gatsby*.' But the play was actually really good. Carey Mulligan played this teacher at this comprehensive – (*Gestures as if to say 'it's me!'*) and she had this speech where she was like really angry at Bill Nighy, who is this older man she used to sleep with and he's shown up out of the blue and is all like 'I still love you.' Anyway, he keeps asking her why she works so hard for such shit money – (*Gestures at herself again*.) and her reply is something like all sarcastic: 'Oh she does it because she's unhappy. She does it because of a lack of confidence in herself. She doesn't have a man. If she had a man, she wouldn't need to do it. Do you think she's a dyke? She must be fucked up.'

I totally get that. When I tell people where I work they think exactly that, I can tell. Even the other teachers who I work with look at me weirdly like 'Why do you have so much energy?' 'Why do you care so much?' Then Carey Mulligan gets really angry and she says, I bought the play and I've read it so many times I know it by heart now. She says – I'm paraphrasing –

She quotes a few lines from Kyra's speech directed at Tom beginning from: '…what the hell does it matter why I'm doing it?' from Skylight, *Act Two, Scene One by David Hare.*

That's what I think. Only… she says it much better than me.

When I feel run down by my job or living in London or whatever I like to think about Carey Mulligan. And it's not to massage my ego and be all self-congratulatory, well, maybe it is – sometimes – but mainly it's to reassure myself that I'm not wasting my life doing something that I'm not passionate about, or doing something that won't make a difference. However tiny it is.

I went to sleep thinking about Kabita and her family.

JOE (*ex-girlfriend*). 'How are you?' She says to me after closing.

'Were you doing Tinder Tuesdays?' I ask, rudely.

'Doing what?'

'That guy was a dick.'

'I know. Thank you.'

There's this pause.

'How's your mum?'

'Moving house. How are you?' I keep fucking fiddling with my sleeve.

She says she's fine. We make small talk. The weather. The pub. The NHS. Then I – I can't help myself. She's smiling and I have this hollow stomach and suddenly I'm saying:

'I miss you.'

Her smile disappears. She closes her eyes as if she's tired.

'Come on. Do we have to do this?'

She crosses her legs a different way. She does that when she's annoyed.

'I'm sorry but you're not nineteen any more. You owe it to yourself to at least try and get your shit together. Stop moaning about how shit everything is. The world is as beautiful as it is ugly.'

STEPH. I woke up with an idea. My phone rang but I couldn't be bothered to answer. There was a voicemail. It was my mum:

'Hiya, sweetheart, just calling to check in, you're probably still asleep because it was Friday night and I'm sure you were out making friends. Do give me a call when you can and we can catch up – I want to hear all about London and what you're discovering. Sal's moving down next Tuesday I think, she's not anywhere near you, though, no, she's got a lovely place near that big Westfield – she says she can see it from the lavvy! Hope you're eating well. We're so proud of you, love. Talk soon. Love you. Bye.'

I found what I was looking for fairly quickly online. I could just about afford it but I'd be eating shit for the next week. But then I was always eating shit cos my rent was so fucking expensive. I sent the guy a message and he replied within minutes.

JOE. As I was walking home from Tesco the following morning I got a – (*Makes birdie iMessage noise.*) on my phone. It was someone who wanted the Xbox. I fucking pegged it home and replied straight away. 'Yeah any time. When do you want it?'

STEPH. As soon as possible / I said

JOE. She said. Sure, of course, I have something to do but meet in New Cross in a couple hours?

STEPH. Can we meet anywhere more central?

JOE. Of course / I said

STEPH. He said. We agreed on the South Bank where that outdoor bookshop is in three hours. I went to get ready.

Lights fade out on STEPH.

JOE. Right. So. Only one thing left to do now.

I started setting it up.

STEPH. As I walked over the bridge from Embankment
I started to second-guess myself. What if Kabita's mum
thought I was totally overstepping and I offended her.
But then I remembered the exhausted look in her eyes and
thought 'I have a good idea.' If the kids play on it for even
twenty minutes a day then she can spend that time relaxing
or learning bits of English or making friends or realising
how clever Kabita is and – I know it's not much, and I know
it's not that ethically sound, and I know it's not going to
solve anything really but I wanted to do something and, for
now, that's all I could do.

JOE. I was sitting on the Bakerloo line for the second time in
the past couple days on my way to meet a girl. I had a little
cry after I got rid of the ghost. Sounds scary dunnit? This
woman with loads of Whole Foods bags gave me a weird
look. The Tube pulled into Waterloo and I got off.

They notice each other.

STEPH. I got there and saw a guy with a big Xbox... box.
I waved awkwardly.

JOE. I saw this girl waving at me shyly. I smiled at her and
walked towards her.

STEPH. He smiled nervously and came towards me.

JOE. Hi.

STEPH. Hi.

JOE. You're –

STEPH. Steph, yeah – and you must be –

JOE. Joe, yeah hi.

Pause.

Well, here you go. Take care of it, please.

STEPH. I will.

JOE. Is it for you?

STEPH. No – it's – it's a long story.

Pause.

JOE. Can I hear it?

Blackout.

End of Part One.

PART TWO

CARA. 'OWH – you are so feckin' shite at this,' my sister says, elbowing me in the leg.

'You want to go out looking like a knacker cos you will if you don't shut your feckin' gob' – I say, givin' the braid a good tug.

'OWH. I never look like a knacker.'

'You do.'

She does.

'What are you doing?' she says pulling away from me and trying to look at the back of her head in the mirror. 'I wanted the other way – the fish one – that one's deadly.'

'Well I'm not doing that.'

Truth is, I don't know how to do it, but she doesn't need to know that.

She starts to fidget uncomfortably at my knees.

'So eh, have you told Dylan yet?' she says, she asks, tentative like.

'Who?'

'Cop on, Cara, you know what I said.'

I concentrate – focusing in on her hair. One. Two. Three. One –

'Cara?'

'What!?'

(*Said as if* CARA *is deaf and dumb*.) 'Dylan.'

DYLAN. There was some fella in front of me who was trying to wheel his bike and eat his chips at the same time. He had his arms sort of linked under one of the handlebars like this – swayin' left an' right. He looked like Cara. Well no – he didn't look like Cara – he had bulging eyes and puffy cheeks and big yellow teeth that hung out of his gob – but he reminded me of her cos of that time she insisted on taking her bike to Sweeney's and then getting so locked she wanted to ride it back...

It was the first time I'd thought about her in a while – that's a lie – but it's the first time I've thought about thinking about her in a while. But I must have been smiling too much walking down the street cos the fella turns to me, head cocked, and stares right through me with these big cross eyes.

'See you there, lad. Can I help you with anything?'

CARA. I told a disgusted Caoimhe that I had to take a shite and while I was on the jacks I thought about texting him. I just thought – I should let him know because – even after everything that's happened – he still – well – Loughlin loved him. He was so pleased we stayed mates after I dropped out of college. And then he was heartbroken when we stopped talking. I think one of the reasons he liked Dylan so much was because he would always agree with him when he'd say shite like 'You have so much to offer, Cara.' Some days I believe him. Them. Him. When I'm walking down the street and I feel all light and I've been listening to something good and my mind is ticking – I feel good then – I feel like I can do stuff. I just have to wait. Wait a bit longer. For Caoimhe to get a bit older, for Ma to sort herself out – for Loughlin to – well, yeah... Fuck it, I pressed send.

DYLAN. 'See you there, lad,' he mumbles again as he wheels off, swaying as his chips leave a little trail behind him.

When I got to the station – seven-minute wait – my phone goes off – (*Makes birdie iMessage noise.*)

It was a text. It was from – it was from Cara.

I had only just gotten used to not checking if every message was from her... It was a short text. Only a line.

'Loughlin's died, drinks tonight at Daragh's.'

CARA. 'HURRY THE FUCK UP,' Caoimhe says banging on the door of the jacks.

'I'M NOT DONE YET,' I say, kicking back at it.

It's gonna be weird without him – Loughlin – around. Although, not that he had that much of a presence. He would sit in front of the telly all day watching *CSI* – 'is *Fair City* not good enough for yer man?' Dyl once asked, messin' like. Pop could get away with being in a room full of people and saying nothing – 'He just likes to sit here and listen,' my aunties would say – living the dream, like.

Dyl got mad at me when I said that –

'Hardly a dream that, Cara, is it?'

Pause.

I flushed.

DYLAN. Loughlin was gas. Everyone thought he was off in some other world – gaga and that – but he wasn't – he was so switched on. I remember when I first clocked he was actually listening to it all. It had been a big one the night before and we were sitting in the back of Peg's car – back when she was still drivin'. Loughlin was in the front and Cara and me – sorry, Cara and *I* – were squished in the back – next to the zimmer-frame thing. She smelt like smokes and sweat from the night before – she smelt bad. But I remember taking a deep breath cos my asthma was playing up and getting this big whiff of her by mistake and just having this impulse to kiss her. (*Smiles a bit embarrassed.*) Anyway – we was chattin' about Mother's Day – it was coming up – and I was saying that even though we work in the same building I feel like I never get to see her properly – my mum – and as I was moanin' on Loughlin said – I didn't even know he was listening, I thought he was just dozing – he suddenly says – 'You should call her when we get back.'

I blinked and looked at Cara. She had her eyebrows raised and she was smiling. I wanted to kiss her again.

'Yeah, all right, maybe I will,' I said.

(*Loughlin.*) 'You should.'

'I will.'

CARA. There was a knock on the front door and I opened it. A little old lady smiles back at me. I didn't recognise who she was but she had the same sorta face as me ma so I just assumed she was family.

'She's not up yet,' I say taking a tray of food from her.

She says something in Irish in this low, kinda kind voice and then just backs out the door... What the fuck?

I fit the food in the fridge quickly cos me hands are tight from all the braiding. The house is quiet, 'cept for the sound of the rain hitting the roof and Caoimhe's music comin' from our room. I tap my phone against my knuckles in time to it. Check it. Nothing.

Ma never liked Dylan.

'Stuck-up Southie. Who would have thought you met a man from Dalkey?'

'We're just friends, Ma.'

Then I remember Loughlin piping up

'Come here to me,' he says, 'Who wouldn't want yer, Cara, who wouldn't want yer?'

Ma snorts.

Turns out a fair few, Loughlin, a fair fuckin' few.

DYLAN. The blue line on my phone flashes, waiting for me to type. I'm perched on the edge of the seat on the Dart – all hunched over cos there's this big fella asleep next to me – and I remember being in almost the exact same position on the arm of Loughlin's chair – and calling me mum. He sat there listening as I told her about what I'd been up to and when I asked if she'd like to do something this Sunday, she said she'd like to – she'd like to very much. And then I got a bit teary. Because I felt loved and because – because I felt spoilt, I guess, for having such a good mum and – I dunno. And then Loughlin reaches out this big shakey hand and puts it on my knee. And I dunno whether it was the hangover or the lack of sleep or just this tiny little gesture but, I swear to youse there were full-on tears streaming down my cheeks.

'Mind yerself would yer,' the now-awake fella says as he straddles me, wobbling off at Sandymount.

I move in to the window seat and rest my head against the glass. Watching as the pretty Dublin houses appear and disappear beneath the falling sheets of rain.

CARA. 'Ah go on,' Caoimhe said, 'It will be good for yer, wouldn't it, Shane?'

'Er, yeah, it would yeah, get out the gaff 'n' that.'

Oh well if Shane says it's alright then I better do it. Shane is my sister's new fella. Shane has bought a new pair of runners for the occasion. Shane is fifteen. They normally walk round lost corners of Tymon Park with their fat frogs and sticky fingers. But today, cos it's a special day 'n' that, they want to go to Stephen's Green and feed the swans. The swans.

The rain's stopped and they're sitting on a wet bench, bodies awkwardly turned in to each other. My sister with her new braid – which got a compliment from Shane – her skinny little legs folded over one another and Shane trying to look real confident, legs spread like his dick's too big, Nike backpack still on – with the K coloured in with a biro.

The swans come around, peckin' at the soggy bread. I think of the children of Lir, being trapped on the water for nine hundred years, forced to look at these two pretending to be comfortable in their half-grown bodies.

I think about how long the rest of the day is going to be.
I think about you.

I turn back to them.

'We'd better head off soon, fellas.'

DYLAN. 'I wouldn't put a milk bottle out in this weather' – my manager says as I hang up my jacket.

I work at the café at the National Gallery. I'm not very good at it – can't count for shite – but my mum sorted it for me – she's a restorer here – so. Yeah.

One thing I do like about working here are the voices – the accents. American in different types. Cowboy and

Californian. Spanish people asking for coffeeee. Brits. Boggers even. Love that. I like guessing where people are from. The easiest is American – you can spot them a mile off even before they speak.

'Aye cos they're fat,' says Connall.

He's from the north and his body matches his voice – like he looks like his accent sounds – slow, ploddy – he's got women's hips and this big doughy face. He's class though – shares his green with me sometimes. He loves this one painting of the Virgin holding baby Jesus. Took me like eight tries of sitting next to him – high out of me mind – before I worked up the courage to ask –

'Why do you like this one so much, Connall?'

He shrugs, takes a deep breath and sighs.

'I think I miss my mommy.'

CARA. 'Leave my phone would yer,' I tell Caoi as I do up my seat belt. She pulls a face and chucks it on the dashboard.

Shane sits in the back seat, talking loudly.

'Yeah so I'll probably jus 'ave a gander round the yard next Friday, 'n' tha jung fell'll be there and it would be good for youse to meet him cos he's been goin' on abou' it. Anyone got a chewin gum?'

'No, Shane.'

We turn down Clare Street – fuckin' one-way system – drive past that cake place where we used to go for my birthday – drive past Trinity. That's where I first met Dyl. First year, first day – five years ago? Yeah, must be. Jaysis.

'Name's Cara. What's yours?' What an eejit, so fucking eager like.

When we first started hanging out I always felt real self-conscious. Like I had dirt under my nails or I had just stepped in dogshite. But then he started cutting out poems for me and lending me books – 'I can't believe you haven't read any Joyce.' And he'd ask me to sing and he'd tell me not to look down when I did. And he always asked about me

mam. And I'd tell him all my woes. And he was so
supportive when I told him I had to drop out of college – he
sat me down and talked it through with me and made that
feeling of panic – like there are books stacking up inside yer
– feel a little less –

'LEFT HERE!' Caoimhe shouts, 'Where's yer head at, Cara?'

DYLAN. I had to stay late after work because me mum was
hosting an event – revealing a painting or something
important. Went to the jacks to change into my nice clothes.
I ran the cold tap and splashed some water on my face –
looked at myself in the mirror. The last time I was wearing
this suit I saw her – seven months ago. I took her to the ball
at college – 'sorry, remind me why you aren't going as a
couple?' – my mum asked as she dropped me off, looking at
their house with a worried face – I don't think she'd ever
been to Tallaght before. 'We're just friends,' I said, kissing
her on the forehead as I got out. And it was the truth – with
all her shite going on I didn't want to make a move – to rock
the boat any more than it already was.

But I wanted her to come with me that night – it was her ball
too. And we had a great night. We danced and drank and got
a bit loosey goosey – avoided all the pilled-up fuckers with
gurning jaws and sweaty upper lips. It was light out till late
so we went for a walk, arms brushing together by mistake.
Went all the way up to The Grand Social. She put her fingers
up, two pints, like that, two pints.

Sat outside in the smoking area. Talkin' close, sweet breath,
bit boozy.

I shouldn't have asked. I really shouldn't have asked.

But I did.

'Do you have any nice memories about ye mum?'

'Of course I do,' she said, frowning.

All right, give us one then.

CARA. Sometimes she used to wake us up at the crack of dawn,
bundle me and Caoimhe up in blankets – sneak us out past Da
– we'd get in the car and drive to the harbour all the way over

in Howth and she would – I remember this *so* well – she
would open up the mirror thing that's on the ceilings of cars –
you know the thing – the mirror –

He nods cos he knows exactly what I'm talking about and
I realise I must be locked so I make an effort to keep it
together for the rest of the story –

And in our old car it would light up when you opened it and
she would put on this lipstick – a neutral colour – me ma was
no whore (I laugh, he doesn't) and right before she closed it
she would wink at me through the mirror. And I just
remember how excited that made me feel – thinking my ma
is so cool – and I remember trying to save that memory in
me mind… So she would get out the car and totter down to
the fishermen who were just coming in from their morning
catch and she would chat with them and flirt with them and
touch their arms real lightly until they would say –

'Alright, lady, der you gaow take this' or 'have another, oh
go on, go on you will.'

I would watch her for a while and then dose off – Caoimhe
would already be fast asleep, her breath blowing what looked
like smoke around the car cos it was so cold – and then Ma
would come back with armfuls of fresh fish and we would sit
with it on our laps which would make us stink for school but
fuck it if we cared.

Then when we got home later we'd have lobsters and cracked
crab and we would feast and she would teach us how to get
the meat from the shells like a lady – all polite and slow – and
then she'd show us how to actually do it – like how the
fishermen do it – and we would eat so much we'd feel sick.
And then we'd go to bed so tired and full and warm.

Lights shift, illuminating both CARA *and* DYLAN*, who
continue to speak directly to audience but occasionally direct
a line across the stage to each other.*

DYLAN. She's not looking at me, tapping her foot on the
ground and taking quick drags of her smoke.

'I'm so sorry, Cara. It was a lovely story – it genuinely was –
I shouldn't have said that it wasn't – '

CARA. 'Just order an Uber would yer?'

DYLAN. 'Please – can't we just talk about this – '

CARA. 'Uber.'

DYLAN. 'Come on, Cara, will you just – '

CARA. 'Uber.'

DYLAN. 'And she won't stop saying it.'

CARA. 'Uber. Uber. Uber.'

DYLAN. 'Okay. Okay. Okay,' I say, getting me phone out. 'Four minutes.' She nods. Satisfied, kinda. But still not looking at me… / 'Cara.'

CARA. 'Cara,' he says to me, all affectionate this time. I ignore him though. Blood boiling. Holding back tears. It could be the drink but it's not just the drink.

DYLAN. 'Jaysis why are you going and ruining a nice night like this? I shouldn't have said that about your ma and I'm sorry but – '

CARA. 'Stop It!' I said. 'Just – can we not – can we just wait for the taxi and can you just let me go home. Please.'

DYLAN. There's a silence.

CARA. 'How long?'

DYLAN. I check my phone. 'Three minutes.'

CARA. Another silence.

DYLAN. 'Do you need to stay at mine?'

CARA. 'Why would I NEED to stay at yours?'

DYLAN. I shouldn't have said that either.

CARA. 'Is my gaff not good enough?'

DYLAN. And suddenly that turns into how I think her ma is a bad ma?

CARA. How I have a tendency towards drink just like her.

DYLAN. How I wish I didn't invite you tonight.

CARA. How you use me and my family as a way to feel better about yourself.

DYLAN. How that doesn't make any sense cos how could her family make anyone feel better about anything?

CARA. How you have no clue what it's like taking care of a family – of taking care of anything.

DYLAN. How you didn't have to quit college you just did it because it was the easy way out.

CARA. How you're selfish and spoilt.

DYLAN. How you embarrass me.

CARA. How if you think you're too good for me then you can just stop trying to save me –

DYLAN. 'Too good for what? What the feck are we even – I – we don't even – we're not even – '

CARA. 'I know we're not.'

Pause.

DYLAN. She's gone all quiet now. No more shouting.

Pause.

CARA. 'How long?'

DYLAN. 'But that doesn't mean I don't want to – '

CARA. 'How long?'

Pause.

DYLAN. 'One minute.'

Pause.

'I want to, Cara, I want to so badly I just – I just –'

CARA. 'Just what?'

Pause.

'Just what?'

DYLAN. I'm about to answer: just nothing. Let's do it. Let's give us a go. I think I love you – let me kiss you – please god let me kiss you.

But then I see her face. And she's sort of shut off behind the eyes. And I realise how many insecurities I must have hit. And I remember what she said to me. And it starts ringing in my ears. And I feel so angry – and so pathetic for being so angry – and before I can go through any of those things the Uber is here. And she gets in. And she slams the door. And it leaves.

I watch the little car on my phone till it gets her home. Then I order another.

We haven't spoken since.

CARA. There's a tap at the car window and I almost shit meself. I look to see who it is, expecting it to be a Gard. But it's only Jane. Jane who takes care – took care – of Loughlin a few times a week for the past couple of months. She's got a new sad-looking dye-job.

'Sweet mother of god! How-are-yer?'

You can tell by her tone of voice she doesn't know about Loughlin. And I'm sure as hell not gonna be the one to tell her.

'Grand thanks, Jane.'

'Ahhh look at youse – two of youse are beauuuutiful, sitting there. You getting on with things now that he's on the mendy mend?'

'Yeah we are,' I say, knockin' Caoimhe before she has a chance to say anything.

'Oh it's hard isn't it, girlos, what to do, what not to do... Fair play to youse though... He's getting dere dough. He is. Ah, Jaysis, god help him.'

'Thanks, Jane, we've got to speed off I'm afrai– '

'I remember how it was with me da's da – funny story – I was just after doing the laundry, right, and I come in... Oh Jaysis, I'm after getting me stories mixed up – that was with Maurice, when he went down to Lucan to look for a place him and Mary's wedding...'

DYLAN. 'I've told you to go and give it back and I won't tell you again,' says a voice – I snap my head around to look for the person it came from – it was a woman, dressed all smart, talking to a kid, who was also dressed all smart.

'BUT I DON'T WANT TO,' the little boy shouts turning away from her.

The woman's obviously embarrassed by her son having this tantrum. She crouches down, voice hushed this time –

'I'm going to count to three and if you don't go by then you are going to get a wallop, mister. (*Spots someone she knows.*) Oh hi, Saskia, yeah fine yeah. (*Turns back to the boy.*) One.'

The boy stares her down.

'Two.'

The boy hesitates.

'Two and a half…'

And before I know it I've made my decision and I'm leaving. Pass me mum on the way out – involved in some important discussion about whether she used tempera or oils in the restoration of – eh! It was Connall's fave.

CARA. 'And then he gets a brick and puts it through yer man's car! Can you belieeeve it, girlos!?' Jane says, *finally* pausing for a breath.

'But youse are well anyway?'

We nod.

'And your mammy? Is she getting a few bob together?'

'Do you want a lift, Jane?'

'Ah no you're grand, I'm gonna get the Luas, I think they're running today. Tanks dough, youse are angels.'

'When will we be next seeing yer, Jane?'

'Tomorra, I'll be over tomorra.'

DYLAN. You know that feeling in November – when it starts getting dark early but it's not quite festive yet and you feel fresh and a little light? That's what was happening to me as I got on the Luas. I pictured myself at the pub – walking in and everyone delighted. Cara pulling me in for a close hug that lasts just a bit too long. Caoimhe running up to me and asking me if I could sneak her a drink. Peg looking at me steadily but kindly, relieved I was back – telling me she had finally quit. And at the end of the evening we would sing for Loughlin and everyone would say that I had 'such a lovely voice' and 'he would have been *so* happy to have you here'. And Cara would stroke my back and slip her hand into mine and then we would find an excuse to wait behind after everyone left and we would be polishing the pint glasses and smiling at each other and then I would slowly reach up and raise her chin to mine and kiss her. And it would be a sweet little kiss but then it would turn into something stronger and I would put my fingers on her shoulder, feel the soft fabric of the strappy top she was wearing –

(*In same voice as Jane*.) 'Oh sweet mother of god would yer let me sit down please?'

CARA. 'We're gonna be fuckin' late feck!'

We're stuck in traffic cos of the fuckin roadworks and the thousands of fuckin buses that seem to never move and the fuckin eejits who drive around Dublin.

'Shut up, Caoimhe.'

'Ah will you feckin' swallow your salty shite, Cara, Jaysis.'

'When did you become such a feckin' knacker, Caoimhe – talking like that.'

'I'M NOT A FECKIN' KNACKER WILL YOU STOP!'

She slams on the dashboard and the glove compartment pops open. I swerved – shocked, like – and was about to scream at her to not be such a feckin' little soith when she let out this howl and burst into tears. Hot, angry tears. I swore under me breath and pulled over round the back of Spar. Some Poles were waiting in line to get their paycheques or something. I didn't know what to do. I didn't know she was so – so affected by it – I reached out to pat her on the shoulder but stopped cos I thought that would be too little a gesture. Just would've come across as fake – like something Ma would do. But she just kept sobbing – her whole body shaking.

So I got out the car and walked round to her side, pulled open the door, crouched down beside her, undid her belt and just put my arms around her. Just sorta held her. Cradled her while she cried. Stroked her back. Said soothing things. Not knowing if that was the right thing to do or not.

And then I thought about you and knew you would know – you would know what to do.

And then I thought about me mammy and I knew you were right – cos – she – she should be here helping me with this. With us. Saving us. And then I felt tears in my eyes ready to join in. And all the years and the memories and the moments… I dunno.

Must have been some sight – two of us wrapped around each other crying our eyes out. Poles lookin over thinking 'where the fuck am I after just moving to'.

Eventually the crying stopped and her hi-hi-ccuppy breath got less shallow. I pulled away from her slowly and looked in her eyes. Big beautiful dark eyes like me da had. She wiped my cheeks to make them dry and then she let out this little giggle.

'What is so funny, girlo?'

She nods at my shoulder where she'd been crying.

Covered in orange make-up.

'Sorry,' she sniffs.

'No bother,' I say all matter-o'-fact as I stand up, brush off me damp knees, walk to my side of the car, get in, put the keys in and look at her –

'You're still a feckin' knacker though.'

DYLAN. 'Yeah – sorry,' I say, shifting my bag so this wagon with a cheap dye-job could sit down next to me. I tried to get back into my plan but I couldn't. It was too choppy. Like, I kept going from dancing with Peg to sneaking a pint for Caoimhe – or was that bad – wouldn't I get in trouble for that? Wouldn't an uncle take me firmly by the shoulder and say – 'I think you should leave, Loughlin wouldn't have wanted this' – no – no – that's not how it will go. And then just as I was getting back into it – the fabric of her dress – it's a dress now I think cos it would be disrespectful to wear a strappy top – your one next to me would move or cough or cross herself as the Luas passed a church – and I would be torn away from the rhythm and forced to start again.

CARA. I make me way through the pub. Check my phone one last time.

Snatches of conversation are falling into me –

'Ah at least he's once again with Grainne now' and 'I didn't think they could afford to hire a place like this, was that her that just walked past me? Do you think she heard me?'

I see Shane with his gangly arm around Caoimhe. She's nestled into him. She looks happy. Safe.

She's got him.

Ma's got her vices...

'For Loughlin' – Daragh – me fat cousin's fat husband says, swaying, red in the face.

But Da's gone.

Everyone raises their glasses – 'Sláinte.'

Loughlin's gone.

Then suddenly I'm being ushered up on stage – 'A song' – everyone shouts – 'Put that college to good use now, Cara,' 'Gis us a song' – 'Loughlin woulda liked tha'.'

And Dylan's gone.

And here I am.

This is it now, I suppose.

For all me days.

This is it.

DYLAN. I get off the Luas quickly, walk through Belgard Square and down to Daragh's. I panic cos the pub looks closed. But then I see this weary-looking little old lady standing outside, as if she's waiting for people to arrive. I think I recognise her. An auntie maybe? No, I don't think so. She looks at me as if she recognises me.

'I'm – I'm sorry for your loss,' I say.

'Go raibh maith agat,' she says in this low, kinda kind voice.

Then there's this sorta pause and as her big, downturned eyes look into mine the death of a man I had grown to love finally dawns on me. Properly, this time.

And I keep staring into her eyes as I realise what a cunt I am.

How selfish I've been.

Today and all the days.

And I feel like she knows exactly what is going through my mind because as she goes in, she leaves the door open a crack – and as I lean against the cold wall, the window ledge digging into me' back – I hear this music drifting out.

CARA *sings the first verse of 'On Raglan Road' by Patrick Kavanagh and The Dubliners.*

I don't think it was Cara – the voice was too sad and low – she had a high, light voice where youse could hear her smile in it.

DYLAN *starts singing on the second verse. After a few lines,* CARA *stops singing, overcome with sadness.* DYLAN *finishes the verse.*

I didn't go in. I can't tell you why. I just didn't. By the time the song had finished I was on the bus home in my fuckin' suit. Tears freezing halfway down my cheeks and my lips all chapped from the cold, Dublin night air.

Blackout.

End.

WRETCH

Rebecca Walker

For Iraj

Acknowledgements

Thanks to Maya Wasowicz, Elle While, Hilary Tones, Calum Callaghan and Valentina Ricci for giving the play its first life; to our first audiences at the Whitechapel Mission, South London YMCA, Dragon Café, Women at the Well, the Spitalfields Crypt Trust, Lifeline Hackney and The Margins Project for their warm welcome and incisive feedback; to Nick Quinn, Jamie Harper, Matt Applewhite, Sarah Liisa Wilkinson and the VAULT Festival team for taking a chance on the play in its transition to the stage; and to Eliza and the Bear for letting us use their wonderful music in the VAULT Festival production.

Special thanks to Tori Allen-Martin, whose talent, passion and badassery has been a candle in the dark.

Last but not least: to the guests, volunteers and green-badges at Crisis at Christmas' Women's Centre, who made my many Christmasses with their compassion, strength and great humour in the face of life's very worst knocks. Thank you for sparking it off.

R.W.

Wretch was created with Maya Wasowicz and Elle White for Into The Wolf Productions, and toured homeless hostels, drug rehabilitation clinics and drop-in centres in 2015, with the following cast:

AMY	Maya Wasowicz
IRENA	Hilary Tones
MIKE/JOSH	Calum Callaghan
Director	Elle While
Designer	Valentina Ricci

It was first performed at VAULT Festival, London, on 8 February 2017, with the following cast:

AMY	Tori Allen-Martin
IRENA	Debra Baker
MIKE/JOSH	Timothy O'Hara
Director	Jamie Harper
Assistant Director	Zoe Sharp
Producer	Tori Allen-Martin
Set Designer	Molly Syrett
Stage Manager	Celia Talbot

Characters

AMY, *a girl from Scotland*
IRENA, *a middle-aged woman from Poland*
JOSH, *a young man from Ruislip*
MIKE, *a man from Cheshire*

Note on Text

(–) indicates a not-fully-finished thought

(…) indicates a trailed-off thought

A speech with (…) in place of written dialogue indicates
a character deliberately responding by remaining silent.

Scene One

Hostel. Kitchen. Two in the morning.

AMY is sitting at the table, wearing a peeling name label reading 'AMY!' in large capitals.

A wash bag and a collection of miniature soap bottles are spread out over the table. She has a permanent marker pen in her hand.

IRENA is wearing a coat, has just come in from outside. A bag over her shoulder.

A fluorescent strip light overhead flickers, pings into light.

AMY looks at IRENA.

AMY. Alright.

> IRENA *half-nods a response. Takes her coat off, puts it over the back of a chair. She is wearing a warehouse uniform – aertex shirt and tracksuit bottoms.*
>
> IRENA *fiddles with the padlock on a locked cupboard, opens the cupboard and takes out a loaf of bread and jam.*
>
> AMY *watches her.*
>
> Midnight feast?

IRENA. Dinner.

AMY. Night owl?

IRENA. Night worker.

AMY. You just back from work? Hardcore.

> *Beat.*
>
> I know you.
>
> IRENA *turns, looks at her.*

IRENA. 'Amy.'

AMY. You remember me?

IRENA. No, you are wearing name label.

AMY *looks down at her top. Pulls at the edge of the sticker.*

AMY. Like starting fucking primary school –

IRENA. You move in today?

AMY. Aye.

IRENA *turns back to the counter, begins to assemble her sandwich.*

AMY *watches her.*

…do you remember me?

IRENA. No.

AMY. What's your name?

IRENA. Irena.

AMY. I never knew that. Where's that accent from, 'Irena'?

IRENA. Jamaica.

AMY. Funny.

IRENA. Where is your accent from?

AMY. You never seen *Trainspotting*?

IRENA. I saw first half. Then I turn it off.
Irish taking drugs, no jobs and fighting all the time –

AMY. – Irish? –

IRENA. I want to see this, I go back to Poland.
Dublin in this film, just like Warsaw.

AMY. Dublin in *Trainspotting* looks like Warsaw?

IRENA. You are from Dublin?

AMY. Apparently.

IRENA. Too many Irish in London.

AMY. Too many Poles.

IRENA. Yes. Too many Poles also.

AMY. You lot love it round here. Polski Skleps on every corner.

IRENA. Not here

AMY. I saw 'em on the way up –

IRENA. Tottenham is Polish shops. Edmonton is mostly Turkish shops.

AMY. Fucking melting pot! What's not to like…

IRENA *returns to her sandwich.*

AMY *watches her keenly.*

I been moving the furniture round my room. The bed was facin' away from the door, so you wouldnae ken if anyone came into the room. I moved it into the middle now, so when I'm in bed I can keep one eye on the door and one on the window. 'Cept the window's got no curtain, so I got the street light shining in.

IRENA. Speak with reception. They will get you curtain.

IRENA *has finished making her sandwich. She shoves it on a plate. Makes to leave.*

AMY. You goin' to bed?

IRENA. Yes.

AMY. You'll not get any sleep. There's a racket going on outside, folks screamin'.

IRENA. No, it is foxes.

AMY. What?

IRENA. Foxes make intercourse in car park. It sounds like screaming. Every night.
You get used to it.

IRENA *moves to leave.*

AMY. You got any tea?

Like, a cup of tea?
Don't mean to be rude but. Not had a chance to get anything in yet.

Beat.

IRENA *puts her plate down on the counter. Sticks the kettle on.*

Bends down to her cupboard, takes a mug and a box of tea bags out of her cupboard.

Had my dinner at Crazy Chicken on the High Road.

You been there?

IRENA. No.

AMY. It was alright.
Well. You know. Chicken shops. They're kind of the same. Bright lights. Chicken.

IRENA. Sugar?

AMY. Aye.

IRENA *digs a bag of sugar and a tub of powdered milk out of her cupboard. Puts them on the table.*

AMY *picks up the carton of powdered milk. Examines it.*

Wha's this?

IRENA. Milk.

AMY *shakes it.*

AMY. It's solid.

IRENA. You want fresh, go to petrol station.

AMY. Is this a Polish thing?

IRENA. No.

IRENA *pours out the tea.*

Puts the mug down on the table.

Fridge in here is like magic box. Everything you put in, it disappears. Powdered milk is better, you can lock it in cupboard.

AMY *tips some – rather a lot – into the tea.*

AMY. Looks like you could shove it up your snout!

IRENA *watches* AMY *as she takes a sip of tea. Takes a bite of her sandwich.*

AMY *looks up.*

You wanna sit down?

AMY *sweeps a space amongst the litter of bottles.*

IRENA. What is this?

AMY (*re: marker pen*). I'm puttin' my initials onta my stuff. The laddie with the mole –

IRENA. Jono.

AMY. Jono gave me a whole box of bath stuff. Said I could choose whatever I want!

IRENA. Everyone gets this when they move in.

AMY. Aye, an' I don't want mine getting mixed up with any other fucker's.

IRENA *sits down gingerly at the table. Puts her sandwich down in the available space.*

IRENA *eats.*

AMY *sips her tea.*

IRENA. This is your first time? 'Amy'?

AMY. First time what?

IRENA. In hostel?

AMY. Yeah.
I went to rehab. Southend-on-Sea.
Then 'emergency accommodation' in Hackney. Worst week o' my life. I was sharing a bathroom with a junkie who'd jack intae the soles of his feet, sitting on the tub. Every time I went in the floor was just this sea of blood – ! But it got me here. Been clean a year.

Can I ask you somethin'?
What's Edmonton like? Never been here before.

Beat.

IRENA. There are dogs. Everyone has dog in Edmonton. You must be careful where you stand, there are everywhere shits on the pavement.

AMY. Okay –

IRENA. There are many shops for ninety-nine pee, good for cleaning products and Toblerone.

Also many gambling shops, African churches...

That's it basically.

AMY. I'm made up bein' here.

IRENA. I will move soon.

AMY. Where to?

IRENA. Private rental. Studio flat.

AMY. You can afford it?

IRENA. I work full time. I save most my deposit.

AMY. You're a good example.

IRENA. Of what?

AMY. For me. Of what I could do.

IRENA *stands.*

IRENA. I must go to bed. Nice to meet you.

IRENA *puts her plate in the sink, makes to leave the kitchen.*

AMY. I saw you a few times. The 73 night bus, last year?

I was there, *that* night.
You don' remember?

IRENA....

AMY....

IRENA. If you have question about anything here, you can knock on my door.

AMY. Thank you...

IRENA. Room B-twelve.

She exits.

AMY *watches after her.*

Goes back to marking her name on to her toiletries.

Scene Two

7 p.m. the following day.

IRENA*'s room. It is spartan except for a row of books and a wooden box on a shelf. Immaculately tidy.*

A hard-house track pumping in the room above.

IRENA, *dressed in an elegant skirt and blouse, is sitting in a chair, reading a book. Seemingly oblivious to the music thumping through the ceiling.*

An incessant banging starts up on IRENA*'s bedroom door.* IRENA *looks up. Removes earplugs from her ears. Goes to the door, opens it.*

AMY, *with a grin, in the doorway.*

AMY. Hello!

IRENA. Yes?

AMY (*re: music, shouting*). I thought that shite was you.

IRENA. No.

AMY. You said knock if I needed anything...

IRENA. What do you need?

AMY. Jobcentre advice!

AMY *thrusts a form at her. Bounces into the room.*

I like your room –

The music switches off abruptly. Footsteps overhead. A door banging.

AMY *looks up.*

– thank fuck for that –

IRENA. Every day between five and seven –

IRENA scans the form. Looks up at AMY.

– Jono can help you with this – ?

AMY. Jono's busy. You know the one always in her bra an' panties?

IRENA. – Marina –

AMY. Aye, Marina. She's out on Fore Street, shoutin' at cars. Jono's out there one hour, tryin' to put some clothes on her, fuckin' hilarious.

IRENA. What advice do you want?

AMY. Just, you know. Jobcentre man said, 'It's all how you present the information.'
Think he's in to me.

IRENA. Why do you think I –

AMY. Cos look at all them books, you fuckin' KNOW shite…!

AMY looks at IRENA *expectantly.*

IRENA. Now?

AMY. You got a pen?

Beat.

IRENA gets a pen from her bag, holds it out to AMY.

My handwritin's wank.

IRENA eyeballs her.

Sits down with pen and form. AMY *perches next to her on the end of the bed.*

IRENA. This will just take five minutes –

AMY. – aye –

IRENA. – what is it you need help with?

AMY. Getting the answers right.

IRENA. This is not exam.

AMY. Yeah, I know, but if we JUST go through it beginning to end we can decide what to put for each one, alright?

Sorry. Shite day.

(*Re: the form.*) Was waiting there three hours. This chav in the queue's wee prick sicked up on ma Nikes.

Beat.

IRENA *looks down at the form.*

IRENA. They want just – CV information. You know what CV is?

AMY. I'm not fuckin' stupid.

IRENA. So. What is your full name?

AMY. Amy Elizabeth Jenkins.

IRENA. Date of birth?

AMY. First of May, 1989.

IRENA *writes.*

IRENA. Education and qualifications –

AMY. Not really.

IRENA. Where did you got to school?

AMY. Kircaldy High School.

IRENA. Where is this?

AMY. Kircaldy. Scotland.

IRENA. You did not go to school in Ireland?

AMY. No.

IRENA. You have no qualifications?

AMY. No.

IRENA (*reading*). 'Employment history for last five years.'

Beat.

AMY. I worked in a market in Glasgow, selling DVDs.

IRENA. Job title?

AMY. …I just sold 'em…

IRENA. 'Market seller'?

AMY. Aye, okay.

IRENA. Employer?

AMY. Frank. Cash in hand.

IRENA. Do you know Frank's last name?

AMY. No.

IRENA (*writing*). Frank… *Jones*.

IRENA. Responsibilities?

AMY. Selling DVDs.

IRENA. Okay, but they want more information, so, did you take any money from customers?

AMY. Aye, took the cash, gave 'em change –

IRENA. Okay this is good, this is responsibility. I will write, 'handling money' – this is good skill.
Reason for leaving?

AMY. Frank got done. All them DVDs were nicked.

IRENA. Okay.

Next one?

AMY. Came down to London. There was a gap. Worked in a pub for a couple of months.

IRENA. Responsibilities?

AMY. Glass collecting.

IRENA. Good.

AMY. That's where I met Mikey, love of ma life.

IRENA. …what happened after this?

AMY. The pub burned down. Insurance job.
Another gap.

Car wash, Croydon. Used to hoover the seats, clean the cars on the inside –

IRENA (*writing*). Car wash. Job title, 'Cleaner'?

AMY. Yeah cleaner. Run by these Romanians, fucking crooks, no offence to you.

IRENA. – I am not Romanian –

AMY. Right. Used to promise me cash that never showed. The whole thing was a cover for a scrap-metal business. The main laddie used to make a mint jackin' copper off the train lines. Used to get me to move it sometimes, thought I looked less dodgy.

IRENA. What happened?

AMY. I started looking more dodgy. That was around the time things started fucking up. Got done for possession.

IRENA. So I will write, 'Car wash, Croydon. Cleaner.' And what – since then?

AMY. Nothin' since then.

IRENA. There is just one more question. 'Write down areas of employment in which you are prepared to seek work.' So, kinds of jobs, or places –

AMY *thinks*.

AMY. Maybe a shop. Like one of them big department stores. Where I can wear a uniform. I'm good at sellin' things. My nana always used to say 'you could sell ice to the Eskimos'.

IRENA *looks at her for a moment. Then writes.*

Beat.

IRENA. This is it. You can sign?

AMY *nods*.

IRENA *hands the form and pen to her.*

AMY *scribbles her signature. Absent-mindedly gets up.*
Goes over to the pile of books neatly stacked on the floor.
Runs her finger along the spines of the books.

IRENA *watches her.*

AMY. Did you bring all of these from Poland?

IRENA. No…

Beat.

IRENA *goes over and joins her.*

I bring with me just two.

And now, each month I buy one new.

AMY *is counting the books under her breath.*

AMY. What's your favourite?

IRENA. It is one that I brought with me.

IRENA *takes a book from the pile. Hands it to* AMY.

AMY. Skinny wee thing

IRENA. It is poetry. Adam Mickiewicz.

AMY. Good, is he?

IRENA. Yes. He's very good.

AMY. You had a massive book with ya, on the bus that night.
Fell off your lap. I put it back in your bag for ya.

Beat.

IRENA *takes another book off the pile. Hands it to* AMY.

This is it?

IRENA. Dostoyevsky. *The House of the Dead.*

AMY. Horror story?

IRENA. No. It is about life in prison, in Siberia.

AMY. Cheerful.

IRENA *looks at* AMY *for a moment, hesitates.*

Then opens the book to a marked page.

IRENA. Listen.

'Man is a creature that can become accustomed to anything, and I think that is the best way of defining him.'

AMY....

She flicks through the volume of poetry. Looks up.

You've written all over it!

IRENA. Yes

AMY. That's bad!

IRENA. No, they are notes for the poems.

Pause.

I used to be teacher.

AMY *looks up at her.*

School teacher. Before I came to England. Long time ago.

Beat.

AMY. When I was sixteen I donated bone marrow to someone. Saw a documentary on TV about leukaemia, late at night. I was fucked but it had me crying my fuckin' eyes out. So I joined the register, spur of the moment, and never thought nothin' would come of it but three months later they found a match. So in I went, I spent two days in hospital, my hip aching like fuck, then I got discharged and kind of forgot about it. And then got this letter a while later, from the mam. And a photo. The kid looked like a fucking ghost but the letter was all like, 'oh she's so much better', and it was all about how the family could do this trip to Italy now and how this kid was buzzin' cos she was really into the Ancient Romans. And at the end of the letter she said, 'whoever you are, and whatever you go on to do, remember that you'll always be our hero.'

Isabella, she was called. She wanted to be a teacher.

IRENA. This is very good thing to do.

AMY. You just made me think of it now.

I dunno.

You were a teacher. You ain't a smackhead or an alkie. And
you ain't stark starin', even if you did try an' top yourself.

Was it cos of your man?

IRENA....

AMY. It's alright, don't need to explain.
He around here then?

IRENA....no. He is in Poland.

AMY. Want me to Megabus over an' fuck him up for ya?

Nah.
I left my man Mikey when they offered rehab. Had to. Only
way I was gonna give it a go. Most lonesome fuckin' year of
my life.

IRENA. This is brave. To choose to be lonely.

AMY. Yeah well.

Don't even know where he is now.

Beat.

Can I ask you a question?
Are you? – Not bein' funny – ?

IRENA. What?

AMY. On the game?

IRENA. – what?

AMY. Sex worker.

IRENA....no – !

AMY. Not bein' funny, just you're always out funny hours.
'At work', creepin' back at five in the mornin' –

IRENA. I work night shifts –

AMY. – that's what they all say –

IRENA. – in warehouse, for things bought on internet! –

AMY. Oh. Right.
You like it?

IRENA. It is okay.

AMY. What do you sell?

IRENA. 'Lifestyle products.'

AMY. Oh.

You gonna go back to bein' a teacher?

IRENA. In England it is not so simple.

AMY. You gonna go home one day?

IRENA. What for…?

AMY *picks up the form.*

AMY (*re: form*). You have been helpful.

IRENA. Good.

AMY. I think, ya know. You put things well.

The door upstairs slams. Footsteps across the ceiling. The music starts up again.

AMY *grins, rolls her eyes.*

IRENA *nearly smiles.*

AMY *makes to leave.*

IRENA (*raising her voice*). Amy?

AMY *turns.*

It was you?

AMY (*loud*). What was me?

The music snaps off abruptly. Silence rings through the room.

Beat.

IRENA. They told me some girl called ambulance – but I did not know who…

AMY. Oh aye.
Yeah. That was me.

IRENA.…

AMY. Wu'n a big deal.
Would've been a fuckin' bawbag if I didnae.

Gonna go computer room now. Got arse to whup on Candy
Crush Saga.
Thanks, yeah?

AMY *exits again.*

IRENA *alone.*

The music blasts out again.

Scene Three

Manager's office, order fulfilment warehouse.

IRENA*'s manager,* JOSH, *sits at his desk.*

IRENA *stands the other side of the desk. She wears a staff
lanyard round her neck.*

JOSH. LaToya.

IRENA. Irena.

JOSH. Sorry. Wrong day.
Windows 10 – bane of my life…!

He clicks through pages on his desktop.

Looks up. Grins.

Irena Stanczuk?

IRENA. Yes.

JOSH *continues clicking through pages.*

JOSH. You're in at number two.

IRENA. Sorry?

JOSH. Second fastest order-to-despatch this week. Well done,
Team Lynx!

IRENA. Thank you.

JOSH. Overtake those Mountain Lions and those ten-pound vouchers could be yours.

IRENA. I have question. You need more staff?

JOSH....we always need staff.

IRENA. I know someone would be good for warehouse.

JOSH. Great. Tell them to go to our agencies –

IRENA. But – not everyone is agency?

JOSH. – we recruit online as well –

IRENA. Perhaps personal recommendation save you time –

JOSH. – I am always open to new warehouse talent –

IRENA. – and better than agency staff who leave two days after they start...?

JOSH. We're not offering contracts –

IRENA. Okay, but. As temp, I know she will stay as long as you need her.

JOSH goes back to his computer, opens his calendar.

JOSH. I don't have much time this week –

IRENA. She is outside.

JOSH. Here?

IRENA. Yes.

JOSH. Now?

IRENA. Yes.

Pause.

JOSH. You don't mess about.

IRENA....

JOSH looks at his watch.

JOSH. I've got ten minutes till my Pret delivery.

IRENA. Thank you.

IRENA exits.

Enters with AMY. AMY *is wearing an ill-fitting long skirt, cardigan and blouse – clearly belonging to* IRENA. *She looks a bit Amish.*

This is Amy.

AMY. Alright.

JOSH. Welcome, take a seat.

AMY sits down in front of JOSH's *desk.* IRENA *hovers nervously in the corner.*

You're looking for work?

AMY. I brought my CV.

JOSH. Let's have a look.

AMY takes a document out of her rucksack, hands it to JOSH.

Looks round at IRENA *for reassurance as* JOSH *reads.*

Amy Elizabeth Jenkins.

AMY. Aye.

JOSH. Twenty-seven. You have GCSEs… six subjects, grades B to D –

AMY. Aye.

JOSH. Including – Palaeontology?

AMY. I like dinosaurs.

IRENA. Amy has passion for customer service.

JOSH. Where was your last job?

AMY. 'Imperial Car Care.'

IRENA. It is company providing valet service.

AMY. 'Luxury vehicles.'

IRENA. It is cleaning for private cars and taxi fleets.

AMY. Irena was the team leader.

IRENA. That's how we know each other –

AMY. In *Knightsbridge*.

JOSH. You're her referee?

IRENA. Yes.

JOSH (*reading*). 'As a Car Care executive, I was responsible for… exceptional standard of customer service… administering full wash, wax and polish… managing client accounts.'

AMY. Yeah, and some clients were dead tricky, with proper high expectations. Expectin' you to polish a jobbie, you know what I mean?

IRENA. Amy always met these expectations –

AMY. 'I am good at working under pressure'!

JOSH. You worked there for how long?

AMY. Six months.

JOSH. And when was this?

AMY (*looking at* IRENA). A year ago?

JOSH. Okay, and what have you been doing for the last year?

AMY. …I went away. On holiday. You know. Needed to clear my head. A detox.

IRENA. A retreat.

AMY. A retreat. *Spain*.

JOSH. Before that you worked at a pub in East London –

AMY. I was a waitress in their restaurant. And I baked stuff as well. Stuff to sell, behind the counter. Baked –

IRENA. – cakes –

AMY. Yeah, baked cakes and biscuits and. Baked potatoes.

JOSH. You were also a customer service assistant at Blockbusters, Glasgow.
What kind of responsibilities did you hold there?

AMY. I checked the DVDs in and out. Stocked the shelves. Stocked them by type of film, you know, horror, romcom.

JOSH. Great.

AMY. Sometimes I'd move it all round. Make up my own sections, like 'Angelina Jolie' or 'Incest'.

JOSH. Right.

AMY. And: I'd call the customers and give 'em hell if they were late bringing their DVDs back.

JOSH. Aha: we *don't* give our customers hell.

AMY. No.

JOSH. They give us hell. The customer is king in the online market. Do you have any idea how many products we stock here?

AMY. Thousands?

JOSH. Around thirty million across our ten UK despatch warehouses. We sell on average fourteen products a second. Irena: what is our top-selling product this week?

IRENA. Jamie Oliver poach egg pan.

JOSH. Ours is not to question why. Ours is to get that pan through despatch as though the survival of civilisation depended on it. Our mantra is Excess. We need to Exceed Expectations. The sooner our shopper gets her egg pan, the sooner she'll come back and spend. Are you and speed on first-name terms?

AMY. Well, not in a couple of years –

IRENA. Amy is very fast.

JOSH. Speed, Stamina, Strength. Irena is one of our fastest operatives, and that's not because she's young and fit, it's because she's got good attention to detail.

JOSH *takes a deck of children's flash cards out of his desk drawer, takes a sub-selection of them, and slaps them down on the desk, one-by-one:*

Birthday cake
Bicycle

Donkey
Windmill
Tomato

He grins.

Gathers the cards up again, shuffles them, hands them to
AMY. AMY stares at him, wide-eyed.

What order did I give them to you in?

Beat.

AMY *looks at the cards.*

AMY. Birthday cake.

She puts the card down on the table. She looks at him.
He looks back at her.

She puts the next card down.

Bicycle.

Donkey

Tomato

Windmill?

Beat.

JOSH. Not bad.

AMY (*elated*). I got a good memory –

JOSH. You switched the last two. But not bad for a first go.

JOSH goes back to his computer, clicks through pages.

Most of our Christmas temps are still with us. How busy
would you think we are in January?

AMY.…not very busy?

JOSH. Why's that?

AMY.…cos everyone's skint from Christmas?

JOSH. You'd think so. But: January is also the month of the New
Year's Resolution. People want to become better versions of
themselves, and they'll spend what it takes to get there.
Yoga mats. Fitbits. Paleo bars. We are exceptionally busy.

JOSH *sits back in his chair. Appraises* AMY.

Great oaks from little acorns grow, and I am proud of my oak. Are you up for being one of my acorns, Amy?

AMY. Yes, definitely.

JOSH. We need staff in Outgoing Post. Post-room operatives are there to sort the items coming out of Packaging into the relevant regional despatch freights.
Sound alright?

AMY. Yes definitely.

JOSH. These are casual contracts. We will offer you available shifts but we are not obliged to offer you shifts, you understand?

AMY. Yes definitely!

JOSH. It works well for most.

JOSH *rifles through papers on his desk.*

He stands. AMY *stands.*

I'll go and grab a new-starter form...

He exits.

AMY *turns to look at* IRENA.

AMY. Did he offer me a job?

IRENA. Yes.

AMY. Do I start now?

IRENA. Not today but, soon.
You are alright?

AMY. Yeah. It's just... this is *big*.
No one's done this for me before...
I'm gonna take you on holiday when I get paid – you seen much of the British countryside? We'll go Center Parcs! An' I'll save for a flat too, like you!

IRENA. – this will take time –

AMY. – paint the walls. Go B&Q! This is my *time*, Irena!

AMY *throws her arms around* IRENA.

IRENA *freezes. Then softens, a bit. Pats* AMY *awkwardly on the back.*

AMY *stands back, holds her skirt out to the side.*

If Mike could see, what do you think he'd fuckin' say to this?!?

AMY *twirls in her ill-fitting skirt. Laughs.*

IRENA *watches her.*

JOSH *returns, clutching a Pret a Manger bag.*

JOSH (*re: Pret*). Ran into him!
(*Handing* AMY *the form.*) Here you go. Fill it in and drop it in at HR. We have new-starter inductions every Monday.

AMY. Thank you.

JOSH (*slapping* IRENA *on the back*). Keep up the good work, Team Lynx.

(*Sitting down, looking in his bag.*) Beetroot and prawn korma. Living dangerously, Pret.

Scene Four

The lounge area of a rehab facility. Visiting hours. Two weeks later.

MIKE *sits at a table.* IRENA *sits opposite. She keeps her coat on, and her bag on her lap.*

MIKE. You're not my aunt.

IRENA. No.

MIKE. Didn't think you would be. She died in Marbella in 2009.

IRENA. I had to think of something. They allow only family to visit.

MIKE. They think all our friends are addicts.

IRENA. Are they?

MIKE (*thinking*). Yes.

IRENA. Thank you for seeing me.

MIKE. It's not every day I get a visit from a fake aunt.
It's not every day I get a visit.

Sorry, but – have we met?

IRENA. No.

MIKE. You gonna put me out my suspense?

IRENA *takes a photo printout from her bag and pushes it across the table.*

MIKE *picks the picture up.*

MIKE. She's dead?

IRENA. No!

MIKE. Thank fuck. Don't push photos of loved ones at addicts, they're always gonna think the worst.

IRENA. She is well.

MIKE (*re: picture*). Where did you get this?

IRENA. She gave it to me. She prints out her photos from Facebook and gives them away as presents. She has given me – ten –

IRENA *takes another handful of photo printouts out of her bag and puts them on the table.*

– I do not know why.

MIKE (*smiling at photo*). Vain little beast.

IRENA. She gave something like forty to key worker, Jono, she pushes them always under his door.

MIKE. Amy has a hard-on for authority figures.

IRENA. A what?

MIKE. You one of her support workers?

IRENA. No. I am friend.

MIKE. How does Mary Poppins become friends with Amy Jenkins?

IRENA. We live together. In the same place. In hostel.

MIKE. You? Who'd've thought.

I'd heard she was housed. She's staying clean?

IRENA. Yes.

MIKE. Behaving herself?

IRENA. More or less.

MIKE. Did she send you to tell me?

IRENA. No. She does not know where you are.

MIKE. And you found me – how?

IRENA. Facebook also. She gave me idea.

MIKE. Alright, Miss Marple –

IRENA. Your profile picture you are standing outside front of rehab centre smoking big cigarette. It did not take detective to find you.

Beat.

MIKE. You gonna tell me why you're here?

IRENA. Yes.

You are getting out from here soon?

MIKE. Four days. You make it sound like prison.

IRENA. It looks like prison.

MIKE. Prison's more fun. There are drugs in prison.

Nah, I'm joking, it's good, I feel good. These guys are so puri-fucking-tanical, they'd put the Mormons to shame. Not even allowed caffeine in the centre, like one Nescafé's gonna make us wanna mainline. If I get offered another lemon and ginger infusion I'm gonna deck someone.

IRENA. Where do you go when you leave?

MIKE. 'Supported Living.' In Beckenham. One house, four addicts and a key worker onsite. That's when you know they really fucking hate you, they ship you out to Kent. It'll be like *Men Behaving Badly*, but shitter.

IRENA. I want to ask. Please do not contact her.

MIKE. Sorry?

IRENA. Amy. Please do not contact her when you leave.

MIKE. Why do you ask that?

IRENA. Her life has moved on.

MIKE. I'm aware of that. I haven't seen her in a year –

IRENA. Yes but. She talks about you.

MIKE. Why do you think I would wanna see her?

IRENA. I don't think, I don't know… anything –
    I just worry about her.

MIKE. She tell you where I met her? King's Cross Station.
    Three year ago.

    She was scabbing off the punters at the ticket machines,
    strung out in a right state. But she was singing to herself an'
    smiling – and there was something sweet about it, like part
    of her mind was miles from there.

    I loved that girl right then. It was like *Fatal Attraction*. No –
    Brief Encounter. That one with the station. Things was bad,
    but she knew how to laugh at herself. She was down but she
    weren't out. She gets by, no matter what.

IRENA. She said she met you working in pub. Before she
    started using.

MIKE. Did she now? Did she tell you I was the start of it all
    going wrong?

    Beat.

    IRENA *takes fifty pounds in bank notes out of her handbag.*
    Puts them down on the table.

IRENA. You deserve fresh start as well.

MIKE. Is this a bribe?

IRENA. It is not easy living on Jobseekers Allowance, when
    you are paying service charge, doing weekly shop… Head
    start when you leave will help.

She pushes the money across the table.

MIKE *puts his hand on top of hers. Squeezes it.*

MIKE. You think you're close to her?

He smiles.

That's our kid's talent. She understands what people wanna see and reflects it back.

IRENA *pulls her hand away.*

'Rough and tough but a heart of gold.' Poor little girl, crying herself to sleep at night?

There's only one thing in her heart, and it's the pull of the next high. And if she's clean, she'll just be lookin' for another kick. Is it you right now?
You think you're the first person's tried to help her? I weren't. She sucks people in then spits them out. She got me hooked… on more than one thing.

She tell you about our son?
My little boy with his blotchy skin, who couldn't stop crying that high-pitched cry? She wouldn't stop, even for him. She was using again, five hours after they took him away, never asked about him again.

She tell you about all those times in hospital, when I sat by her bed thinking, 'This is it, this is goodbye.' And she'd come round and smile that sweet smile and then we'd start all over again?

You think you know her?

Middle-aged dyke, is it?

IRENA. Sorry?

MIKE. Fucking lesbian?

IRENA. No.

MIKE. – wouldn't've thought you were Amy's type, but then as we've said, she's unpredictable –

IRENA. – I *owe* something to her –

Beat.

MIKE. Darling. You don't know what you're in for. It's you that should stay away from her.

IRENA *stands*.

MIKE *stands*.

Going so soon?

IRENA. Will you do what I ask you?

MIKE. I'll let you in on a secret.

I weren't gonna fuckin' go there. She walked away when she got clean, and fair on her.

He puts the cash in his pocket.

But – thanks for the gift, auntie. See ya.

He blows a kiss at her.

Exits.

Scene Five

Manager's office, order-fulfilment warehouse. The next day.
JOSH *sits at his desk.*

AMY *stands the other side, wearing the same warehouse
uniform seen on* IRENA *in Scenes One and Three.*

JOSH. Two weeks?

AMY. Aye.

JOSH *looks at his computer screen.*

JOSH. Eight shifts.

AMY. Actually it's been nine, one of them was a double –

JOSH. – mm-hmm –

AMY. 6 p.m. to 6 a.m., full-on all-nighter…

JOSH. Would you like to sit down?

AMY. Yeah.

> AMY *sits. Jiggles her leg up and down.*

> JOSH *looks up from his computer screen. Smiles. Sits back in his chair.*

> AMY *grins back.*

JOSH. You enjoying the work?

AMY. Lovin' it. Sampson's a legend –

JOSH. Sampson – ?

AMY. The supervisor? Proper banter there.

JOSH. Right. Good.

AMY. You know he was a doctor in Eritrea?

JOSH. I didn't know.

AMY. Meetin' people from all over, like – Pakistani, Sudani,
   I never even knew Eritrea was a place, sounds like a disease –

JOSH. Here's the thing, we've been having some problems with
   despatch this week –

AMY. Right.

JOSH. – I'm speaking to everyone in the team, not just you.

AMY. What kind of problems?

JOSH. I know that –
   (*Looks at the screen again.*)
   – Sampson –

AMY. / Yeah.

JOSH. Sampson spoke to you on Tuesday?

AMY. He's a legend, aye –

JOSH. He spoke to you about the fact you were getting parcels
   into the wrong despatch bags?

AMY. Oh, yeah it was just I wasn't sure about the system at the
   time –

JOSH. We've got thirty different sub-regions we despatch to. If things go in the wrong van it can take two, three days to retrieve them and get them turned round. It's not good for Complaints, it's not good for the brand.

You remember what I told you about acorns?

Despatch is my oak tree. I am in charge. But my oak is just one in a large orchard and I am accountable to the other trees. If my acorns are rotten, I don't just endanger my oak, but the orchard as a whole. And that's not good for me.

Still. Sampson's reported no misdirected parcels in the last four days.

AMY (*brightening*). I'm on it now.

JOSH. You're confident you know what you're doing?

AMY. Aye, confident. Everything's tip-top.

JOSH. Now, something else has come up you might be able to help me with.

Customer Complaints have logged a high number of calls reporting missing deliveries in the last, three or four days. The strange thing is – First Class, Second Class, Special Delivery – there's no particular logic to what is and isn't getting to its destination.

AMY. You think someone's nicking 'em?

JOSH. I don't think someone's nicking them. Because if our packages were removed from the building through any door other than the despatch dock they'd set off the alarm.

AMY. Well that's good news.

JOSH. But they have gone missing.

AMY....

JOSH. Can you shed any light?

AMY. Everything looked normal to me.

JOSH. Looked or looks?

AMY. It… looks.

JOSH. No concerns about any of the other post-room executives?
It's not telling tales, you know.

AMY. No, I know. No concerns. No.

He looks at her.

Pause.

JOSH. Okay.

He stands.

AMY *stands.*

It's not good for results, but sometimes these things happen –

AMY. – Yeah, and you know, we got trolleys an' trolleys goin' up and down the whole time and all I'm sayin' is – things fall off.

JOSH. Sorry?

AMY. I saw an Xbox go flying yesterday, the guy didn't even see it, didn't even go back and get it.

JOSH. Which guy?

AMY. I dunno.

JOSH. How did you know it was an Xbox, when everything going out of Despatch is already boxed and packaged?

AMY. The shape.

JOSH. Really?

AMY. Aye.

JOSH. Rectangular?

AMY....yeah.

Beat.

JOSH. Just say your theory was correct. That things were falling off trolleys. Getting lost that way.

AMY *nods.*

Falling off trolleys in a corridor with straight walls, and a solid lino floor.
Where do you think they would disappear to?

No secret trapdoors, as far as I know.

AMY. No. That is bizarre.

JOSH *picks up a printout lying on his desk, hands it to* AMY.

JOSH. These are the orders that have gone missing.

AMY *looks at the page.*

Can you remember handling any of these items?

AMY *looks up from the page.*

AMY. No.

JOSH. How about the addresses on the orders? Any of them ring a bell?

AMY *looks back down at the page again. Shakes her head.*

AMY. No.

JOSH. Couple of quirky places on there. 'Royal Artillery Mansions'. 'Windings Cottage'. A place called Mousehole. They're the sort you might remember.

AMY *shakes her head.*

Amy.

What is the closest address on that list to here?

AMY....

JOSH....

AMY. The London one?

JOSH. Four of them say London.

Geography not your strong point?

Pause.

JOSH *opens a desk drawer. Digs through papers, removes one.*

He comes round the other side of the desk, leans against it.
Hands the piece of paper to her.

AMY. What's this?

JOSH. You tell me.

She looks at it.

AMY. My CV.

JOSH. How can you tell?

AMY. It's got my name on it.

JOSH. Well done. Can you remind me how many GCSEs
you've got?

AMY. Six?

JOSH. Which subject did you get a C in?
It was only one of them.

AMY. I don't remember, it was a while ago now –

JOSH. You don't need to remember. It's written on that piece
of paper.

Beat.

AMY *looks down at the CV. Her hand is shaking.*

AMY. Geography?

JOSH. That's not what it says there.

AMY. Computer Technology?

JOSH. How can it be Computer Technology, it's not even two
words. Read what's written there.

He watches her.

No?

I can read it backwards, through the paper. It says English.
You got a C in English.
Although judging by this display I kind of doubt that
that's true.

AMY *lifts her head, wipes her eyes with the back of her
hand.*

AMY. You said energy was what mattered.

JOSH. If you can't even read, what else on there is true?

AMY. I got a can-do attitude –

JOSH. Did you think I'm stupid? Did you think I wouldn't notice?
Where are the packages?

AMY. I don't know.

JOSH. You've stolen them.

AMY. No.

JOSH. You're completely unfit for this kind of work.

AMY comes close to him.

AMY. I just need to learn.

She kisses him.

JOSH. Is that right?

AMY undoes a button on his flies.

AMY. I just need someone to teach me what to do.

She undoes another button.

Because deep down –

She kisses him again –

I'm a good girl.

AMY breaks off the kiss, looks at him for a reaction. He doesn't react.

AMY gets down on her knees.

JOSH moves away from her, back behind his desk.

Sits down. Does up his flies. Looks at her.

AMY stands, shaky.

JOSH. If you could read your contract you'd know that that, just there, is a sackable offence, too. So now you've got at least three problems, haven't you?

Leave your lanyard at the front desk.

Scene Six

IRENA*'s room. Forty minutes later.*

IRENA *wearing her outside coat and bag.*

AMY *loitering in the open doorway, a package behind her back.*

AMY. Present for ya.

> AMY *takes the package out from behind her back. It is wrapped in old magazine paper.*
>
> *She presents it to* IRENA.

IRENA. What is this?

> IRENA *unwraps it. It is a Billy Bass – one of those novelty singing fish heads.*

Oh… thank you –

AMY. I wanted to get you something for your room.

IRENA. Amy, I must go. I have news –

AMY. You off to work?

IRENA. No, Jono has flat for me to see. I have now enough in deposit, the rest Jono says can be interest-free loan – I go see it now –

AMY. You moving out?

IRENA. I think so. I mean, yes, unless it is complete shithole. But Jono says he thinks it will be nice. It is studio. You want to come with me?

AMY. Nah.

IRENA. – I go to work after –

AMY *(re: Billy Bass)*. Call it a housewarming present then.

> *Pause.*

IRENA. You are okay?

AMY. Just a bit cold.

IRENA. It is like sauna, whole building –

> *Pause.*

AMY. Can I stay in your room?

IRENA. Why?

AMY. My room's cold. The radiator's gone wrong.

IRENA. Did you speak to reception?

AMY. There's no one down there.

Can I stay in here? Just while you're out?

Pause.

IRENA. Okay. Yes. Of course.

AMY *hugs her. Holds her too tightly.*

She kisses IRENA.

Beat.

Kisses her again. It's a bit too intimate.

IRENA *gently detaches herself. Regards* AMY.

Beat.

AMY *goes over to* IRENA*'s bed, climbs under the covers.*

Turns her face to the wall.

IRENA *sits down on the edge of the bed. Strokes her hair.*

You are not well?

AMY. I'm just cold.

IRENA. You have had dinner?

AMY. No.

IRENA *looks at her for a suspended moment.*

Pause.

Then goes over to the box on her shelf. AMY *turns to watch her.*

Takes out a twenty-pound note.

IRENA. You can get takeaway.

AMY *sits up. She hugs the duvet to her chest like a child's blanket.*

AMY. Thank you.

IRENA. Indian or something.

AMY *smiles.*

IRENA *ruffles* AMY*'s hair. Heads for the door.*

AMY. I'll get a chicken jalfrezi. Save you the leftovers.

IRENA (*exiting*). I have sandwich.

AMY *left alone. The room is quiet.*

AMY. I'll save you something anyway.

Scene Seven

AMY*'s room. Hostel. Twelve hours later.*

The door is wide open.

The room is piled high with random objects in their new wrappings, including a cuddly leopard, a designer egg whisk, and an open packet of birthday balloons.

A number of inflated balloons litter the floor. They all read '4 Today!'

AMY *is rooting through the debris on the floor.*

AMY. – It's got to be in here somewhere –

IRENA *appears in the doorway. She stares at* AMY. *Stares at the pile of objects.*

She picks up the cuddly leopard. Looks at it for a moment.

IRENA. Amy –

AMY *swings round. Wired.*

AMY. Oh, you've met my leopard – !

IRENA. What is this?

AMY. He, not what. His name's Bruce.

IRENA. What is – all this – ?

AMY. I'm throwin' a party. You're invited.

IRENA. These things are from work?

AMY. Yeah, used my staff discount.

> AMY *is rooting through the pockets of her clothes, bags, drawers…*

> I lost it.
> No, no. It's not lost, it's just fucking –

> *She runs her hands through her hair.*

> You've just got to think –
> What my nana used to say –

IRENA. Amy, my door is open –

AMY. I'm sorry, I'm a bit distracted right now –

IRENA. When did you leave my room?

AMY. I dunno, when I woke up?

IRENA. Did you leave the door open?

AMY. Not really sure.

IRENA. Can you think?

AMY. I dunno, Irena, could've done. I'm a bit fucking scatty like that.

IRENA.…What are you looking for?

AMY. My bird, my neck chain with the wee bird on it –

IRENA. – Why is this so important?

AMY. Because he gave it me, and he'll want to see me wearin' it –

IRENA. *Amy.*

> AMY *stops searching, looks at* IRENA. *She is sweating.*

> The money is gone.

AMY. What money?

IRENA. Five hundred fifty. From my box. In my room.

AMY *stares at her.*

IRENA *stares back.*

AMY. All of it?

IRENA. The box is empty.

AMY....

IRENA....

AMY. I'm sorry, Irena, but I really need to find this chain –

IRENA. You took it?

AMY. Fuck off.

IRENA. *You took it?*

AMY. Why would I wanna do that, huh, when I've already got all these *things* –

AMY *picks up the electric whisk.*

– you got any eggs? Cos I can whisk the fuck out of them whenever ya want –

IRENA. You take these from work?

AMY. Aye I took 'em.

IRENA.... Why?

AMY. Because here's the truth: I needed a leopard in my life.

AMY *grabs the leopard off* IRENA, *lies down on the floor and cuddles up to it.*

IRENA. You stole –

AMY. – Relocated –

IRENA. You *stupid* girl –

AMY. Aye, you're right. I am really *fucking* stupid –

AMY *throws the leopard at her.*

YOU FUCKING SET ME UP, you know that? –

IRENA. – What?

AMY. 'It's just takin' things off the shelves.' Turns out to be a lot fuckin' more than that –

IRENA. What are you talking about?

AMY. 'Really fucking easy' you said –

IRENA. Amy –

AMY. I CAN'T READ THE LABELS.

Aye. That's right. Can't read. Pretty much at all.

I could do some, the ones I recognised the postcodes...
I had to hide the other ones.

IRENA. This is them?

AMY. Not all of them. Some are in my locker, but then it got full. So I brought these ones home. Left the packaging in the bins in the lav so that the alarm wouldn't go off.

IRENA. They will find out.

AMY. They already have.

Beat.

AMY *chucks a balloon skin at* IRENA.

– You gonna blow that up or what? –

IRENA. You should have told me, I would not have got you this job –

AMY. Aye? What job would you've got me instead?
What do you think I'm suited to?

IRENA. Amy. I said yes to flat.

AMY. Congratulations (!)

IRENA. I will sign papers tomorrow. I will pay deposit tomorrow.

IRENA *grabs* AMY *by the shoulders, pulls her up.*

Where is my money?

AMY. You special needs or summat, keepin' money in your room?

IRENA. Where is it?

AMY. 'Indian takeway'? Fucking neon sign, flauntin' it –

IRENA. You are using drugs again?

AMY. Nah, I'm high on love.

   No drug beats that. Made all the sweeter when you been apart.

IRENA.... You saw him?

AMY. Not yet – he gets out this afternoon, but we conversed on the telephone. And he had a good wee tale to tell, about his auntie from Poland, flashin' the cash, givin' him money to stay away.

   She turns on IRENA.

   Who the fuck are you, playin' with *my life*?

IRENA. I did this for you –

AMY. No. You did it for you. He's the only one in the whole world – yeah we had our goods and bads – but the only *real thing* I ever had – and you *told him to leave me alone* – ?

   AMY *picks up one of the objects from the pile, smashes it across the room.*

   IRENA *grabs her by the shoulders.*

IRENA. I did it to help you –

AMY. What the fuck is your *interest*? A teacher, with all your books? I'm sorry if this is news to you, but we're from different fucking planets –

IRENA. You tell me? I am so *stupid* –
   I spend one year avoiding every woman in this place, hiding from this storm of fighting and screams and crying, every moment, every day. And I have no pity, I *despise* them because every little thing that is done to help them they bleed, and shit and vomit away. And you? You are the same –

AMY. – True, true –

IRENA. You are just *junkie* – drug addict, nothing honest, no integrity, same as the rest. You have no heart, you are like this *Groundhog Day* movie, every day this gerbil and same story –

AMY. – It's a *groundhog*, you fucking fool, that's why it's called *Groundhog Day* –

IRENA. Where is my *money*? This is my deposit for flat – I will move, next week –

AMY. Aye I know, the amount you been banging on about it – but *You Don't Wanna Go* – that's the truth.

IRENA. *No* – you have not spent it yet –

AMY. – You don't wanna go cos then you'll be *all alone*.

Beat.

IRENA. I know you have not spent it.

AMY. Ah well no, you're wrong there. That's what smackheads do. Seize the day and all.

First I got a 'starter' with that twenty quid you gave me. But then I thought, fuck it. I'll get a bit of rice *and* curry.

You want a breakdown of what I spent it on?

IRENA *sinks to the floor in tears*.

One twenty on smack.
Another hundred on crack, to get the party started.
Two seventy on settling a bad debt. Thanks for that.
And another forty on meth. Not really my thing but Mikey's got a fondness for that racy high.

I've not done it all at once, you'll be pleased to know. Just enough to take the edge off till he gets here. He'll be made up seein' his auntie.

IRENA. What do I do now? What do I *do*?

AMY *grabs at her*.

AMY. You stay here with me. I done you a favour.

She holds her tightly. For a moment IRENA *is limp*.

Don't leave me alone.

IRENA *shrugs her off*.

IRENA. No. Next week I move –

AMY. How you gonna raise that deposit on seven fifty-five an hour, huh? Gonna take you – I dunno – *a year* to save –

IRENA. – How could you? –

AMY. You could go on the game, it's a good way to make a quick buck. Although maybe not at your age –

IRENA. Get out.

AMY. You're in MY ROOM.

IRENA. This is *my home*. It was okay before you come, get out, you make it *stink* –

AMY. I'll be gone soon enough.

IRENA. You think because the world doesn't give shit about you you can do what you want?

I work at this stupid job and every week another new face, another stranger, never a friend, never someone to get to know. I work there just to pay for this place, this – mental hospital – on *moon* – so far from anywhere, where no one comes, just poor and crazy people who have no choice, where noise never stops but you are always alone. And I tell myself, it don't matter, keep working, you can block everything out. Why am I blocking life out?

AMY *is staring at her, glassy-eyed. Her breathing is laboured.*

I left my husband, I left my life, because I was not safe. I came here because he had no passport and it was all I could think. I could not think beyond staying alive.

But wanting to stop is not always unhappiest thing. It was clear thought, that night. Like looking into cold water.

And then I wake up in hospital, in so much pain, and they tell me, 'something wonderful happen'. Someone found you, someone called ambulance for you. Someone saved your life.

You can live without love… but you cannot live without *hope* of it. So if I have to live –

I keep going, because this stranger, this unknown person told me to…

AMY *sits down on the floor.*

AMY. That was your mistake. Listenin' to me.

IRENA. What is point when everything hurts, and there is no happiness, nothing to make it better?

AMY (*mumbling*). I got happiness.

IRENA. Not here.

AMY *itches her arms, she is sweating.*

AMY. Out there.

IRENA. You have ruined my life.

AMY. Thought I saved it.

IRENA. I wish you didn't.

AMY *hugs her arms over her stomach, bent double.*

AMY (*faint*). Wanted to matter to someone.

IRENA. I wish you didn't.

AMY *sinks on to the floor. Her head droops.*

IRENA *watches.*

Doesn't move.

Scene Eight

A recovery ward in A&E. The next day.

AMY *in a hospital bed, hooked up to an ECG monitor. She is pale, her hair lank against her face.*

MIKE *enters. Similarly pale but on his feet.*

They look at each other.

MIKE. Too Much Too Young.

AMY. Fuck off –

MIKE. This gotta be a first. Normally it's me can't keep up with you –

AMY. Aye, well, I had a head start this time.

MIKE. How you feeling?

AMY. Fuckin' joyous.
   How long we been here?

MIKE. Eighteen hours.

AMY. Were you – ?

MIKE. No. I done my coming down in the waiting room, sittin'
   opposite a man with a screwdriver stickin' out of his thumb.
   Not missed this, I can tell ya.

   Time was, we could've had a loyalty card for this place.

AMY. What do you get when you've got ten stamps? A free
   rock?

MIKE. This in't funny.

   Beat.

AMY. Did you bring me in?

MIKE. I called the meds – don't remember much after that –

AMY. You shouldna. I would've been fine –

MIKE. Ame, you had a fucking seizure. Sick all over the Circle
   line.

AMY. We was on the Tube?

MIKE. Yeah

AMY. Why?

MIKE. You wanted to go Tower of London.

AMY. I would've been fine.

MIKE. Great, I'll leave you to die next time.

   Beat.

   There won't be a next time.

   Beat.

AMY. Does my hostel know?

MIKE. Yeah, the nurse called them.

AMY. What did they say?

MIKE. She wouldn't tell me. Is it one strike and you're out?

AMY. Shouldn't think so.

MIKE. This is serious.

AMY. First offence. It'll be fine.

What about you? House of Fun have you back?

MIKE. Jimmy said they love a relapse.
Key workers get all excited handing out leaflets, gives 'em a new reason to live…

But I'm not going back.

Gonna go up north.

AMY. You what?

MIKE. Decided, sittin' out there. Starin' at an advert for Peak District cottages in *Good Housekeeping*, made me feel homesick.

AMY. Fuck off.

MIKE. Gonna try family mediation.

AMY. Family – fuck off – ?

MIKE. Know it wasn't up to much last time. My angry brother and a fat woman in a turban handing out Kleenex. Weren't much of a peace process.

But still.

This in't working.

AMY. Comedown blues –

MIKE. I mean it.

AMY. Your life's here.

MIKE. That's the problem.

You didn't need this. I didn't need this –

AMY. We was always alright together –

MIKE. Got a cousin in Stockport, he said I could stay a while,
spoke to him a few days before / you showed up

AMY. I think we should go back.

MIKE. You're not coming with me –

AMY. No, I mean –

Back out there, Mike. We're better skipping.

Keep getting texts off Dodger. You know Rex died, had
a tumour?
And Steph's back, back from Brighton, wants to hook up –

We was alright out. Things was better –

MIKE. – Thought you changed your number. How you even in
touch?

AMY. I changed it back.

MIKE. You're fucking mental –

AMY. You didnae think so last night –

MIKE. Yeah well.

He looks at her.

Moment of weakness.

Beat.

Last night don't change nothing for me. And you've had
a year.
How could you want to go back?

AMY. Because I'm homesick…

MIKE *holds his hand out. She takes it.*

MIKE. Comedown blues.

AMY. Aye.

He kisses her hand.

Beat.

MIKE. I'm gonna go.

AMY. Stay –

MIKE. Nah. Now I know you're alright –

> Don't like the smell of this place.
> You gotta sort this out with them lot at the hostel.

> AMY *hesitates. Nods.*

> You should call 'em. Sooner the better. You're gonna have to go crawling.

AMY. Don't worry. Jono loves me. Pictures of me all over his room.

MIKE. Behave yourself with them key workers.

AMY. I know, aye. I will.

Scene Nine

McDonald's, Central London. Morning. One month later.

IRENA *sits at a table, drinking a coffee, reading the* Metro. *She has a plastic bag beside her.*

AMY *the other side of the window. Sees* IRENA.

Comes in, approaches the table. Stops.

IRENA *senses the presence. Looks up, sees her.*

Gathers her stuff, gets up quickly to go.

AMY. Don't go –

IRENA. I have finished–

AMY. You only just sat down.
Saw you through the window.

> *They look at each other.*

> IRENA *sits down again.*

> AMY *straddles the chair opposite.*

> Fancy seein' you here…

IRENA....

AMY....Never seen you here before...

IRENA. Why should you?

AMY. This is my McDonald's.

Errol, Employee of the Month, slips me an apple pie now and again. Says it's just the ones that fall on the floor, but no one drops that many apple pies. You want one?

IRENA. – No –

AMY. Hey, Errol!

IRENA. I do not want one.

AMY. Oh. Okay.

Let me get you another coffee then.

AMY *digs around in her jacket pocket. Deposits a handful of coins on the table.*

Got fifty, sixty....
One pound ten?

IRENA....

AMY. Is it enough?

IRENA. I do not want another coffee.

AMY. For later, then.

AMY *pushes the coins towards her.*

IRENA *looks at the pile. Does not touch it.*

How's the hostel?

Beat.

IRENA. New woman in your room.

AMY. What's she like?

IRENA. She does not say much.

AMY. Nice change for you.

IRENA. She bangs on my door in middle of the night, she always thinks she can smell fire.

AMY. Smell smoke. You smell smoke, not fire.

IRENA. Yes.

AMY. …At least she's trying to get you out.

Beat.

How's work?

IRENA. I am not there any more.

AMY. Cos of me?

IRENA. No.

AMY. Good

IRENA. I left.

Beat.

AMY. So now you're just – hangin' round McDonald's?

IRENA. No, I have new job.

AMY. Oh, that's good.

IRENA. Polish nursery, in West London.

AMY. You're teachin'?

IRENA. Not teaching. Nursery assistant.
Jono made me contact Polish Women's Association.

AMY. That's good. More Poles in your life.

IRENA. No, it's not. They want to know everything.

AMY. But good you're teaching again.

IRENA. It is only two days a week. So I will be in the hostel
some time longer.

Beat.

You sleep here?

AMY. 3 a.m. till 7. After the clubbers, before the office workers.

AMY's phone rings. She answers it.

Aye, alright?
Nah, it weren't open. It weren't open!

You gonna be around later?

Meetin' Daff in Islington at three. Somethin' like that.

AMY *looks up at* IRENA.

I'm takin' tea with a friend just at the minute.

I'll fuckin' kill him if he don't. Aye, he better. Give him a kiss from me.

See ya later.

She smiles. Hangs up.

(*To* IRENA.) Pal's birthday. Tryin' to sort out a cake. You know them ones shaped like a caterpillar?

IRENA. Mike is with you?

AMY. Nah, he's gone up north.
Matter of time before he's back, though.

Beat.

IRENA. I must go.

AMY. Wait, Irena?

Got somethin' I wanna show you.

AMY *roots around in her bag.*
IRENA *watches her.*
AMY *digs out a very scrunched-up piece of A4 lined paper.*

Did this workshop at the day centre? 'Poetry'. Didn't wanna go but it was either that or friggin' 'Sew Your Own Washbag'.

So aye, I wrote a poem.
I mean, I thought it up an' the tutor wrote down the words.
Took all fuckin' afternoon, kept redoing it.

And now I can't remember it all.

AMY *shoves a bit of crumpled paper at* IRENA.

IRENA. I read it?

AMY. If you want to...

IRENA *unfolds it. Looks at the page.*

Beat.

IRENA (*reading*). One rainy day I found a bird
  Its wing was broken, it looked absurd

  I took it in, I fed it worms
  I brushed its feathers till it had no germs

  Slowly this bird was feeling better
  It stayed with me, whatever the weather

  Then one day the sun came out
  My well-fed bird started to sing and shout

  I wanted it to stay with me.
  Share my home and share my tea

  But then I knew, if it was love
  Then I must let it fly above

  My bird flew off into the night
  It really was a lovely sight

  It turned around to wave at me
  And I was happy as can be.

AMY (*happy*). It's shite, innit.

IRENA. It is not shite.

AMY. True story, you know. Found a seagull, few years back,
  outside Aldgate Station. He didnae fly off though, the
  RSPCA came and took him away in a transit van.

IRENA. Amy, I could teach you to read.

AMY. What?

IRENA. We could meet here. Once a week or something.

  Starting with this?

AMY. I don't think so –

IRENA. Why not?

AMY. ...I've tried –

IRENA. You could try again.

  It is not too late.

AMY. I know you want to think that.

I'm alright, you know.

Pause.

IRENA. I must go –

She gathers her things to leave.

AMY. Where to?

IRENA. Nursery. There is child there, he is building house for snails from shoeboxes. It has become small castle now – (*Smiles.*)
I promise him today we will make drawbridge.

She indicates her plastic bag, containing a shoebox.

AMY *nods.*

IRENA *starts to exit.*

AMY. I don't want you to feel bad –

IRENA *stops.*

IRENA. I don't feel bad. You are responsible for you.

IRENA *continues to exit.*

AMY. You'd regret it –

IRENA. What?

AMY. Teaching me...

IRENA *turns back.*

IRENA. This is probably true.

They look at each other.

AMY. My nana did used to call me 'a late bloomer'.

IRENA. What does this mean?

AMY. I dunno.
Something good?

Black.

THIS MUST BE THE PLACE

Brad Birch & Kenneth Emson

This Must Be the Place was first performed at Latitude Festival
on 16 July 2016, with the following cast:

ADAM	Mike Noble
LILY	Molly Roberts
TATE	Feliks Mathur
MATTY	Hamish Rush
Co-Directors	Justin Audibert
	Josh Roche
Stage Manager	Susan Burns
Sound Designer	Kieran Lucas
PR	Chloé Nelkin Consulting
Producer	Poleroid Theatre

The play transferred to VAULT Festival, London, on 8 February
2017, with James Cooney taking over the role of Adam.

With thanks to Corinne Salisbury and Rosa Crompton.

Poleroid are a new-writing theatre company encouraging
multi-disciplinary work and artist development. They believe
that people learn through doing and set frameworks for artists to
showcase and develop their skills in a supportive environment.
They explore the dark undercurrents of life in the twenty-first
century from the perspective of those on the margins whose
stories we rarely get to hear. They give a platform to exceptional
fast-rising new writers, actors and directors from across the
UK and through our collaborative method nurture bold urgent
new work that is committed to engaging new, younger audiences
with theatre.

www.poleroidtheatre.co.uk

Characters

ADAM
LILY
TATE
MATTY
MAN
WOMAN

The unallocated lines at the beginning, before Adam speaks,
can be spoken by anyone in the cast.

This is not a London story.

No timely tale of protests on the street.

Nor night-bus-puke recollections.

No rising rents and financial complaints.

No.

None of that here.

No bankers, nor hipsters, nor tourists who just
don't know where the fuck to stand on an escalator.

This is not a London story.

Though it does start in London...

He stands.

And he could be us.

Or us him.

There is a quality.

One we recognise.

And that thought crosses his mind too.

How very alike we all are.

How similar.

Let's call him Adam.

Just to give him a name.

Something for us to remember him by.

So Adam stands on Hungerford Bridge and looks
down the winding river that weaves its way
through the capital city. The lights, the offices, the
banks and tower blocks, the flats owned by Russian
and Saudi businessmen who only visit once a year.

It is summer.

And the day is slipping silently into night.

There is a nip to the air. A summer nip.

On another night he might have regretted his choice of H&M vest top and skinny jeans, the plimsolls, the half socks that will leave no tan line.

So maybe there are hipsters in this tale after all.

But Adam isn't really one of those people.

He just wears the uniform.

To fit in.

To conform.

To disappear.

But tonight.

Tonight with its nip.

He is very much here. Very much present.

He can feel it.

Life.

Everywhere.

All around him.

He is halfway down the bridge...

ADAM   I.

Not he.

Let's say I.

I am halfway down the bridge, past the beggars, the *Big Issue* sellers.

I am leant against the rail.

Occasional couples walking past turn to see me. They have a look of worry on their face.

Doubt.

Fear.

They have seen these things before. Either on television or in films. In fictional stories in the books they have been bought for Christmas by parents who don't read blurbs.

But this fear. This doubt.

It is contagious. You can see it in their eyes.

Could it be happening here?

Even here?

An iPhone is in my hand. Like so many iPhones.

I imagine there are iPhones in hands right now. Right here. Even in this place where the reception is weak.

Even when they should be turned off rather than switched to silent.

But there is a chance of a message, a text, a tweet, a post, a new status.

A connection.

A name.

Adam stands.

I stand.

But in a way.

We.

We all stand.

And for the first time we start to feel the weight of it.

The iPhone.

The device they rent us for a small and not-too-inconveniencing fee per month.

This door to another world.

A world of every piece of information we could ever want at the touch of a button.

Every image.

Every sound.

Every memory.

Of kitten memes and terrorist attacks and thoughts and feelings and wrongs and rights and opinions and drunken rants we'll regret tomorrow when we read them back in the cold light of day.

This distraction.

This distance.

I shut my eyes. Take a breath. And let it drop.

The amputation of a limb.

The loss of a parent.

The conversation as we part.

The fading light.

An ending. A beginning. A new.

Hi. This is Adam. I'm not around at the moment. Please leave a message after the beep.

Beep.

Hi. This is Adam. I'm not around at the moment. Please leave a message after the beep.

Beep.

Hi. This is Adam. I'm not around at the moment. Please leave a message after the beep.

Beep.

LILY   Has anyone seen Adam? He's not picking up his phone and I'm starting to worry.

ADAM   Hi. This is Adam. I'm not around at the moment. Please leave a message after the beep.

Beep.

LILY   Hi Adam, it's just me. I've left you about ten missed calls and texts. Can you ring me when you get this?

ADAM   Hi. This is Adam. I'm not around at the moment.
         Please leave a message after the beep.

         Beep.

LILY   Adam, this isn't funny. Ring me.

ADAM   Hi. This is Adam. I'm not around at the moment.
         Please leave a message after the beep.

         Beep.

LILY   I swear to god if you come home smashed I am
         going to be so pissed off with you.

ADAM   Hi. This is Adam. I'm not around at the moment.
         Please leave a message after the beep.

         Beep.

LILY   Adam, I'm scared. Call me. Please. I'm really
         worried about you.

ADAM   Hi. This is Adam. I'm not around at the moment.
         Please leave a message after the –

LILY   Where the fuck have you been?

ADAM   What?

LILY   Where the fuck have you been?

ADAM   Well, that's a nice thing to say when I walk in the –

LILY   Adam, where the fuck have you been?

ADAM   Out.

LILY   *Out.*

ADAM   Yeah. Out.

LILY   Out, out?

ADAM   No. Just out.

LILY   It's nearly midnight. I've been trying to ring you.

ADAM   I lost my phone.

LILY   Did you leave it in a pub? You left it in a pub didn't
         you? I knew –

ADAM   I didn't leave it in a pub. I haven't been to a pub.
         Why is that always your first –

LILY   You smell of alcohol.

ADAM   I had one after work. Okay? That's not a crime.

LILY   I didn't say it is.

ADAM   Good.

LILY   So where is it?

ADAM   What?

LILY   The phone.

ADAM   I lost it. I don't know. That's the problem with
         things that are lost. You don't know where they are.

         A silence.

         Sorry.

LILY   Don't say sorry unless you mean it.

ADAM   I am sorry. I should have let you know.

LILY   You haven't been online all day. I was worried.

ADAM   And I consider telling her. I really do.

         Because I think I actually might love her.

         If that is a thing. A real thing.

         Heart emoji.

         But I don't.

LILY   I'm going to bed. I can't be arsed with this. I thought
         we were going to watch *Game of Thrones*. That's
         what you said. I was looking forward to it all day.

ADAM   Lily...

LILY   Yes?

ADAM   A vein collapses. A monitor flatlines. A door closes.

         Nothing. I'll be up in a minute.

At precisely four in the morning I slip out of bed, lifting her arms from around me gently to stop her from waking.

LILY   Mmmmmmmmmmmm.

ADAM   She makes a noise, but she is still unconscious. Dreaming dreams of midgets and naked people fighting over a fictitious kingdom in a story that will continue to be told long after its author has died of obesity or old age.

We live forever.
Trapped in a screen.
A picture.
A share.
A like.
A post.
A page.
A comment.

She smiles.
It hurts.

I open the front door and pause for a second. I take a breath. An actual breath. It sounds like some nonsense you'd read in a book. But people actually do take breaths before they do something.

Something different.

We are so similar.

Adam.

I.

We.

Us.

In the downstairs hallway the bike that has always irritated me is sat leaning against the wall blocking half the space. I think the couple on the fourth floor own it. I don't know them. Their names.

They won't miss it.

***

Night-time.

The forest.

TATE *and* MATTY *are sat.*

TATE   Bruce Forsyth?

MATTY   Yeah.

TATE   Fuck off.

            Beat.

            Really?

MATTY   Yeah.

            Beat.

TATE   Bruce Forsyth is not Mickey Dawson's dad.

MATTY   He is.

TATE   He's old.

MATTY   So?

TATE   What do you mean, 'so'?

MATTY   So what's it got to do with anything? You can still
            be a dad if you're old.

            Beat.

TATE   What about the chin?

MATTY   What do you mean?

TATE   Doesn't have the chin, does she?

MATTY   Well. She's got a bit of a chin.

TATE   If it's true then why doesn't anyone talk about it?
            If Bruce Forsyth was really the dad of someone at
            our college then people would talk about it all the
            time. It's like knowing Neil Armstrong and never
            talking about the moon.

MATTY   Mickey keeps it quiet. Doesn't like talking about it.

TATE   Then how do you know?

MATTY   I saw them together, didn't I? Bumped into them.

TATE   What, Mickey and Bruce /

MATTY   / Her dad, yeah.

TATE   Where?

MATTY   Argos.

TATE   Argos in town?

MATTY   Yeah.

TATE   Bruce Forsyth doesn't live in town.

MATTY   No, he must've been visiting.

TATE   How often does he visit?

MATTY   Well I don't know, do I? I don't know the ins and the outs of it. I saw them once.

TATE   Alright, alright. I'm just asking.

         Pause.

         What were they doing in Argos?

MATTY   Buying a barbecue.

TATE   What were you doing in Argos?

MATTY   Getting a sleeping bag. New sleeping bag.

TATE   Right.

         Pause.

         You're not fucking with me now, are you?

MATTY   No.

TATE   Because if you are then you're a prick.

MATTY   I'm not.

TATE   It's just so stupid, lying about Bruce Forsyth being Mickey's dad.

MATTY   I'm not lying. Why would I lie about something like that?

         Beat.

TATE	So you're just in Argos and she says 'oh here's my dad'.
MATTY	Yeah. Basically. She seemed a bit embarrassed about it to be honest.
TATE	What did you say?
MATTY	I just said hello.
TATE	Hello?
MATTY	What can you say?
TATE	Right. Yeah.

Pause.

Actually, when you think about it, she's got a right chin on her.

MATTY	Yeah.
TATE	Good game, good game.
MATTY	Yeah.
TATE	Fucking Chinny Chinny Bang Bang.
MATTY	Cat On A Hot Chin Roof.
TATE	Chin The Night Garden.
MATTY	The Adventures of ChinChin.
TATE	Alladchin.
MATTY	Doctor Chinn Medicine Woman.
TATE	Jaws.
MATTY	Jaws?
TATE	Yeah, like her jaw.
MATTY	Oh right, yeah.
TATE	Jaw out here.
MATTY	Yeah, no, I know. I just thought we were doing chins.

TATE   Yeah, but...

          Pause.

          Wonder what they do for Christmas.

MATTY   What do you mean?

TATE   Like, do you reckon she goes to his for Christmas?
          No offence to Mickey's mum but you would,
          wouldn't you?

MATTY   Ah no.

TATE   No?

MATTY   No, I doubt that very much.

TATE   Why's that?

MATTY   Well, Bruce Forsyth. He's Jehovah's Witness,
          isn't he?

TATE   He's not.

MATTY   He is. Doesn't do Christmas.

TATE   Bruce Forsyth is a Jehovah's Witness?

MATTY   Big time.

          Beat.

TATE   You're a prick. You know that, don't you?

MATTY   Why?

TATE   You're a prick. Jehovah's Witness. He's not
          fucking Jehovah's Witness. He's not fucking
          Mickey's dad at all, is he?

MATTY   Ah, no he's not.

TATE   You're taking the piss.

MATTY   Yeah.

TATE   You're a prick.

          MATTY *laughs.*

I'm glad you amuse yourself.

Beat.

Argos. I knew it when you said Argos.

MATTY   No, you didn't.

TATE   I did. Sleeping bags with Bruce Forsyth.

MATTY   No, I was there for the sleeping bag. Bruce Forsyth was there for the barbecue.

TATE   No one was fucking there for anything, Matty.

Pause.

I've even met Mickey's dad.

MATTY   You what?

TATE   I've met Mickey's dad. Met him years ago.

MATTY   You didn't.

TATE   Yeah. He's a fucking bricklayer or something.

MATTY   Brilliant.

Beat.

TATE   Why do you do that?

MATTY   Do what?

TATE   Just make shit up like that?

MATTY   Dunno.

TATE   It's weird.

MATTY   It's not weird.

MATTY *checks his phone.*

TATE   He's not called yet then?

MATTY   No. Not yet.

TATE   What time is it?

MATTY   Still a bit early.

TATE   Bloody hell.

MATTY   What's wrong with you?

TATE   Well, it's cold, isn't it?

MATTY   Oh. Are you cold, mate?

TATE   Yeah, I'm freezing.

MATTY   Are you, mate?

TATE   Yes. I said I am.

MATTY   I'm very sorry to hear that, mate.

TATE   Yeah, well it's... Oh piss off.

MATTY   Really, mate. I very really am.

TATE   Come on, you must be cold too.

MATTY   Do you want your Pride of Britain Award in the post or in person?

TATE   I want it shoved up your frozen bloody cock hole, mate.

    Beat.

    Why are we meeting him here anyway? It's a bit out the way, isn't it?

MATTY   He says it's less out of his way than actually coming into town. The one-way system and all that. I don't know.

TATE   One-way system. We had to trek up here so he doesn't have to drive a bloody one-way system?

MATTY   I didn't think it'd be such an arse ache. It's nice up here, in the day.

TATE   Is it?

MATTY   Yeah. I used to come up here quite a bit, you know.

TATE   Who with? Sophie?

MATTY   No, no. After Sophie. I used to come up here on my own.

TATE   On your own?

MATTY	Yeah.
TATE	And do what?
MATTY	Have a think.
TATE	What about?

Beat.

Here, I've got bloody mud all in my shoes and worms all up my arse, mate.

MATTY	You already had worms up your arse, mate.
TATE	Got cocks up your arse, mate.
MATTY	Been looking up my arse, mate?
TATE	Tried to but it's just full of cocks, mate.
MATTY	Oh that's handy for you. If you're looking for cocks, mate.
TATE	Like a box of sausages your arse, mate.
MATTY	Bet you haven't seen that many cocks since your dad's birthday, aye mate?
TATE	You remember my dad's birthday, do you? Bit gay that, mate.
MATTY	Nothing wrong with being gay, mate.
TATE	Yeah, but…
MATTY	But what?
TATE	(*Can't think of anything.*) Ahhh, fuck.
MATTY	Brilliant.

Beat.

Two-nil.

TATE	How's that two-nil?
MATTY	Forsyth. And that.
TATE	Bullshitting me about Mickey Dawson and chatting cock. Those aren't goals, mate. They're fucking… fouls. I should have two freekicks.

MATTY   Makes no sense, that.

TATE   Yes, it does. Two freekicks.

MATTY   You keep knocking it out for a throw in. You have a shot and it goes out for a throw in every time. The fucking Emile Heskey of banter.

TATE   Heskey was good. Low centre of gravity. Couldn't knock him over.

MATTY   That's handy for you if the game's about not falling over, but last time I checked the game is about scoring fucking goals.

TATE   You explaining football to me, mate?

MATTY   Feels like I need to, mate.

Beat.

TATE   Did he say this bit specifically?

MATTY   What's that?

TATE   Where he's picking us up. Did he say to come to this bit specifically? Because, well, it's all the same in the dark, isn't it? What if we're in the wrong place?

MATTY   No, this is it.

TATE   How do you know? He could be waiting for us half a mile up that way.

MATTY   No. There's nothing up that way.

TATE   There's fuck-all up this way.

MATTY   Well, apart from us.

***

ADAM   The night is cold.

              The city feels different now.

              Clean.

              For a moment I consider that all of this might be
              madness.

              Have I lost my mind?

              Myself.

              But the steady roll of the bike's wheels feel like
              they are leading me somewhere.

              Towards some kind of purpose.

              And I know this is right.

              Hi. This is Adam. I'm not around at the moment.
              Please leave a message after the beep.

              Beep.

MAN   Want another?

ADAM   I need to –

MAN   One more won't hurt.

ADAM   I'm late.

MAN   A half?

ADAM   Fuck off, I'm not going to have a half am I. Go on.
              One more.

              Fresh pints appear.

              Cheers.

MAN   What's her name?

ADAM   What does it matter to you?

MAN   Coz I wanna know.

ADAM   Lily.

MAN   Would I like her?

ADAM   How the fuck should I know?

MAN   She nice?

ADAM   Yeah. Yeah she is.

MAN   She treat you well?

ADAM   Yeah.

MAN   Then of course I would.

ADAM   Well it's great to have your blessing. That's all I've ever been after.

MAN   You don't have to be cruel. Not any more.

ADAM   Why not?

Hi. This is Adam. I'm not around at the moment. Please leave a message after the beep.

Beep.

The roads are starting to become smaller after I pass the M25.

I can see trees and fields and greenery and life. Actual life.

I don't know where I am.

I've been heading north now since I left the flat.

Maybe four or five hours ago.

Maybe longer.

I don't own a watch.

My phone. My phone was my only clock.

I am outside time.

The sun is starting to rise in the distance.

I considered stopping at a Little Chef for a fry-up.

But somehow I feel okay.

I feel right.

This is right.

The direction.

I pass through small towns and villages.

Greens and woods.

Fields and parks.

Life.

Actual life.

LILY   I just want to have the conversation.

ADAM   Now?

LILY   Well when would you like to talk about it?

ADAM   When I'm less hungover.

LILY   If it was up to you we'd never talk about anything.

ADAM   I'm not saying that Lily.

LILY   I just... We're not getting any younger.

ADAM   Speak for yourself.

LILY   I want to have a family. I want to have a family
            with you.

ADAM   Shouldn't we get a cat first?

LILY   Fuck you.

ADAM   I'm serious. Isn't that what you do? To test-run it?

LILY   To test-run what?

ADAM   Us. If we can do it. Be parents.

LILY   What, so if we don't kill a cat then we can be
            parents?

ADAM   Well there should be something shouldn't there.
            Some fucking test. I had to do a test to be able to
            drive a car, but I don't to raise another human
            being? How the fuck is that –

LILY   Look. I know you have a difficult relationship with
            your –

ADAM   I don't want to talk about that.

LILY   I'm just saying we don't have to be like that.
We can be better than that.

ADAM   Lily...

LILY   I love you.

ADAM   I love you too.

LILY   Then think about it.

ADAM   I will.

MAN   You won't.

ADAM   I will.

MAN   You won't.

ADAM   Don't look at me like that.

I will.

I promise.

I...

Eventually my feet start to give up.

My legs.

So used to only walking the five minutes from my flat to a Tube. And back.

I don't know where the fuck I am.

Some field somewhere.

Outside the city.

I sit down.

I'm hungry.

So hungry.

I wonder if Just Eat will deliver.

Deliveroo.

Then I realise I don't have my phone.

Maybe this is how we become extinct.

Not an alien invasion or nuclear war.

We all just starve to death waiting for our phone's battery to charge.

Hi. This is Adam. I'm not around at the moment. Please leave a message after the beep.

Beep.

We are so similar.

So connected.

I.

We.

Us.

I see the station on the horizon.

How long has it been since I was here?

How long since I saw it?

Since I even considered it?

This gateway.

Home.

Hi. This is Adam. I'm not around at the moment. Please leave a message after the beep.

Beep.

MAN	You still support Tottenham?
ADAM	No.
MAN	You used to.
ADAM	I was like ten years old.
MAN	It was still a disappointment.
ADAM	Loads of them in the England team now.
MAN	And where's that got us?
ADAM	I liked the colour of their kit.
MAN	A proper reason for supporting a team, that.
ADAM	I was ten years old!

MAN	It was yellow.
ADAM	I like yellow.
MAN	Colour of cowardice.
ADAM	You're going to talk to me about –
MAN	You go?
ADAM	Where?
MAN	To the games. Now you live in London.
ADAM	No.
MAN	Thought you would as you're so close now.
ADAM	I'm busy.
MAN	Doing what?
ADAM	Stuff. Life. My life. Okay.
MAN	You don't have to convince me.
ADAM	I know I don't.
MAN	You only supported them to spite me.
ADAM	Seems fair enough.
MAN	Watch out for that car.
ADAM	What car?

The sound of a car screeching to a halt can be heard. ADAM *stares straight forward, a rabbit in the headlights.*

There is a stillness.

Then...

LILY	I just don't want you to regret this.
ADAM	I won't.
LILY	You can't say that.
ADAM	I just did.
LILY	This might be the last chance you get to say...

ADAM   Goodbye.

Your adopted city.
Your adopted life.
Your job title you don't really understand.
Your Facebook profile you spend more time with than your family.
Your Twitter account.
Your place of work.
Your hour-long commute.
Your tweets to the local council about unjust parking tickets.
Your overpriced coffee.
Your air pollution.
Your check-in at the hip restaurant.
Your point of view on world events.
Liked.
Commented.
Shared.
Your individuality.
Liked.
Commented.
Shared.
Your chesty cough.
Your black snot.
Your anxiety on the Tube.
Your worries about a terrorist attack.
Your nice and liberal news articles.
Liked.
Commented.
Shared.
Your mask.
Liked.
Commented.
Shared.
Your mask.

MAN   It's not you.

ADAM   Your family walks over the park.

MAN   That's not you.

ADAM   Your family walks over the park.

MAN   You can say it all you want. But it's not you.

ADAM   Your family walks over the park. Arm in arm.
            All smiling and laughing. Enjoying spending this
            special time together. Enjoying each other's
            company. Your children in the arms of your
            parents. Three generations. Together.

            Hi, this is Adam. I'm not around at the moment.

MAN   FA Cup final. 2006. Steven fucking Gerrard.

ADAM   Best day of your life.

MAN   It was meant to be.

ADAM   You said you'd be back.

MAN   I was coming back. I was.

ADAM   Nah you weren't.

MAN   It was over. Three two down with ninety minutes
            on the clock. We'd lost. I was just about to leave.
            It was over. It was almost over.

ADAM   You stayed.

MAN   Everyone stayed. Penalties. Can't walk away
            before the penalties.

ADAM   And after?

MAN   I can't even remember the night.

ADAM   Was it worth it?

MAN   She kicked me out.

ADAM   You left.

MAN   I didn't leave she kicked me out.

ADAM   Shared.

MAN   I'm a fuck-up okay? A fuck-up. I know that.

ADAM   Liked.

MAN   It wasn't just that day. It was lots of days. Lots of
            games. Lots of pubs. I know okay. I fucking know.

ADAM   Commented.

MAN   I just wanted to see you.

ADAM   Shared. Liked. Commented.

MAN   Before.

ADAM   Shared. Liked. Commented.

MAN   Please.

ADAM   Shared. Liked. Commented. Replied.

MAN   I know how you feel.

ADAM   Shared. Liked. Commented. Replied. Tagged.

         Emoji. Sadface.

         Someone has added you.

LILY   Adam. See what he has to say. Please.

ADAM   We are so connected.

         Accept friend request?

         Accept?

         Do you know this person?

         Report as spam?

         You have been tagged in a post.

         Allow on your time line?

         Allow on your time line?

         Allow?

LILY   Has anyone seen Adam? He's not picking up his
         phone and I'm starting to worry.

ADAM   Hi. This is Adam. I'm not around at the moment.
         Please leave a message after the beep.

         Beep.

         I jump the barriers at the train station.

         A small rule to break.

         Fuck it.

                              ***

They are sat.

MATTY   What did Jenny say?

          Beat.

TATE   About what?

MATTY   About what. About the rapid decline in the form of
Yaya Touré. About what. I mean about this, you
going away.

TATE   Nothing.

MATTY   She said nothing?

TATE   No. She…

          Beat.

MATTY   Did you tell her?

TATE   No, I didn't. I didn't tell her, no.

MATTY   Shit, mate.

TATE   What's shit mate?

MATTY   The situation.

TATE   Yeah, well… You don't make things less shitty by
adding more shit on top, do you? That just makes
a shit cake, a cake of shit.

          Beat.

          Are you purposefully trying to piss all over the
mood or what?

MATTY   No. Not particularly.

TATE   Come on. We should be, like, raving. We should
be… You know, I've never done anything like this.
I've not been anywhere. And now we, together, are
moving to London? It's mental.

MATTY   Yeah.

TATE   Where'd you say this flat was, again?

MATTY   Whitechapel.

TATE   Whitechapel. Sounds fancy that. Really posh.
          Where have I heard of Whitechapel before?

MATTY   Jack the Ripper.

TATE   Oh. Yeah. That's it.

          Beat.

MATTY   I think it's come a long way since then though
          mate. I imagine so. London, isn't it? Everywhere's
          posh now.

TATE   Yeah.

MATTY   So they'll have done it up.

TATE   Yeah. You're right.

          Pause.

          What's the first thing you're going to do?

MATTY   What, when we get there?

TATE   Yeah.

MATTY   Oh mate, I don't know. What do you mean?
          Reckon we're going to be hungry.

TATE   No, I don't mean like right away, I mean like what
          you want to do on your first day.

MATTY   Oh right.

          Beat.

          Work, hopefully.

TATE   Work?

MATTY   Yeah, don't you?

TATE   Yeah but like say we've got a few days before the
          work starts.

MATTY   I can't afford a few days before the work starts if
          I'm honest. I'm skint.

TATE   Yeah. Well, yeah. Obviously. But, you know.

          Beat.

MATTY   What are you going to do?

TATE   Dunno.

            Beat.

            Go to Camden.

MATTY   Why would you go to Camden?

TATE   A girl I met at Isle of Wight Festival said she
            worked at Camden Market.

MATTY   So you want to find this girl?

TATE   Yeah. Or someone like her, at least.

MATTY   Need some money for that mate.

TATE   Yeah. Suppose.

            Pause.

MATTY   What was she called?

TATE   Sylvia.

MATTY   Sylvia in Camden. Sounds hot, mate.

TATE   Ah yeah. Mate, it's London. Everyone's got to
            be hot.

MATTY   Right. Really?

TATE   Well, girls have to be anyway.

MATTY   Yeah.

TATE   For guys it's like… not the same.

MATTY   Yeah. You think?

TATE   Deffo.

            Beat.

MATTY   That's a relief, isn't it?

TATE   For you.

MATTY   More for you.

TATE   For you, Elephant Man.

MATTY   For you, you fucking binbag.

TATE   For you, you shitty bellend.

MATTY   For you, you fishy fanny.

TATE   For you, you...

MATTY   Ahhhhh.

TATE   Fuck off.

Beat.

MATTY   Three-nil.

TATE   Free kick.

MATTY   Throw-in.

TATE   Offside.

MATTY   Yellow card.

TATE   Red card.

MATTY   Relegated.

TATE   Fuck off.

Beat.

MATTY   Maybe Sylvia's got mates and they can take us out.

TATE   Yeah. Maybe.

Beat.

Definitely.

Pause.

Did you ask him whether it matters if I've ever painted and decorated before?

MATTY   No.

TATE   No it doesn't or no you didn't ask?

MATTY   No I didn't ask.

TATE   Ah fuck, why not?

MATTY   I dunno.

TATE   Why don't you know? Fucking hell, mate. What if
          he doesn't want me? I don't know what I'm doing.

          Beat.

          Matty?

MATTY   It'll be fine, man. I shouted for you and he's fine
          with that. We get on. He trusts me.

TATE   Yeah, but I don't want to fuck it up. Will he train
          me up, do you reckon? Like, let me practise
          painting or something first?

MATTY   Yeah, I'm sure he will.

TATE   Will you ask him?

MATTY   We can ask him on the way, when he picks us up.
          Can't we? It's not like we're in a fucking rush. It's
          not like it fucking changes anything right now,
          does it?

          Beat.

          Does it?

TATE   No.

MATTY   No.

          Beat.

TATE   When he fucking gets here.

MATTY   Yeah.

TATE   If he fucking gets here. What's wrong with the lazy
          cock-shaft?

MATTY   He's on his way.

          Beat.

          And I'd pack that in around him, by the way. Just
          a tip.

TATE   What do you mean?

MATTY   When he gets here, talking like that, calling him things like a lazy cock-shaft.

TATE   I'm just saying he's late and if he's late then he's fucking late.

MATTY   Yeah but... He wouldn't like it.

TATE   Yeah, well I don't like him being late.

MATTY   Yeah but you're not a nasty cunt.

          Beat.

TATE   Right. Is he...

MATTY   Nasty.

TATE   A nasty painter and decorator?

MATTY   Can be a nasty anything if you want to be.

          Beat.

          Besides, I don't think painting and decorating is all he does.

TATE   Right.

          Beat.

          What else do you reckon he does? Or should I ask him that when he gets here and all?

MATTY   I wouldn't.

          Beat.

TATE   How did you meet him?

MATTY   Met him when I lived in Manchester for a bit.

TATE   And you met him doing what?

MATTY   Bit of this and that.

TATE   Bad stuff?

MATTY   No. Like, scrapping and that.

TATE   He's a scrapper too?

MATTY   Yeah.

TATE   He's a painter and decorator in London and
        a scrapper in Manchester?

MATTY   Yeah and whatever else.

TATE   What do you mean, 'whatever else'?

MATTY   I don't know, mate. But he does a lot and I don't
        want to know.

TATE   I want to know. If I'm staying in his flat I want to
        know what he does.

MATTY   Well if you find out then don't tell me.

TATE   Jesus, why are you even doing this then if this
        guy's such a nasty cunt?

MATTY   Because it's a way out.

TATE   Flushing yourself down the toilet is a way out too
        but we're not doing that. Bloody hell, what have
        you got me in to?

MATTY   You don't have to come. I didn't make you come.

TATE   Fucking hell.

        Beat.

        Still. Still, still, still.

        Beat.

        How big's the flat anyway?

MATTY   Don't know.

TATE   Suppose we might have to kip together for a bit.

MATTY   What do you mean?

TATE   Like while we get our shit sorted. Before we get
        our own place.

MATTY   But why would we have to sleep together?

TATE   In case the flat's only got one spare room.

MATTY   Oh right.

TATE   Do you know what I mean?

MATTY   Yeah. Yeah, I didn't think of that.

          Beat.

          MATTY*'s phone buzzes.*

          They look at each other.

                         ***

ADAM   For the first five minutes of the journey I'm
          paranoid I'm gonna get caught.

          Fined.

          Kicked off.

          But I am outside rules today.

          I am alone.

          Without recourse.

          So I rest my head against the seat.

LILY   Adam.

ADAM   What?

Lily   Wake up.

ADAM   Why?

LILY   You were having a nightmare.

ADAM   Was I?

LILY   Yeah.

ADAM   Sorry.

LILY   You don't have to say sorry, stupid. Come here.

ADAM   I was just... I –

LILY   You look upset.

ADAM   My dad. He was in it.

LILY   Do you want –

ADAM   No.

LILY   It's okay if you want –

ADAM   I don't want to talk about it, Lily.

LILY   Okay.

ADAM   We are so connected.

         So far apart.

         So very far apart.

         Hi. This is Adam.

LILY   Let's just go back to sleep then.

ADAM   I'm not around at the moment.

LILY   Adam. Please call me. I'm worried about you. I just
         want to know you haven't done anything stupid.

ADAM   Please leave a message after the beep.

         Beep.

MAN   You should ring her back.

ADAM   I lost my phone.

MAN   No you didn't.

ADAM   Okay. I dropped my phone in to a river.

MAN   Deliberately.

ADAM   Yeah.

MAN   Smart move.

ADAM   Fuck off.

MAN   Insurance won't pay out on that.

ADAM   I don't care.

MAN   Say that in ten months' time. Twat. You know her
         number anyway though, right?

ADAM   No one knows anyone's numbers now. It's not 1996.

MAN   You do.

ADAM   I don't.

MAN   Try.

ADAM   I don't know her number okay.

MAN   Try.

ADAM   Fuck off.

MAN   Just try.

ADAM   07.

MAN   That's the easy bit.

ADAM   07704.

MAN   You see.

ADAM   07704668.

          We hide these things.

          Deep down inside.

          07704668225.

MAN   Call her.

ADAM   I will.

MAN   When?

ADAM   After.

MAN   After what?

ADAM   The conversation as we part.

          The fading light.

          An ending. A beginning. A new.

          An ending.

          A beginning.

          I get off the train and a few of the other passengers look at me funny as I vault the ticket gate.

          Fuck them.

          I walk out into this place I know.

This place I have always known.

This place I left.

I walk up to the first car I see on a quiet street and put my elbow through the window.

It smashes with ease.

A trick I learnt here in this very town fifteen years ago.

Muscle memory.

It starts with the application of two wires snapped out and fused together.

A connection.

I drive slowly and steadily through the streets.

Past houses I once sat in.

Pubs I once drank in.

Beds I once fucked in.

Past people I once knew.

Ghosts.

MAN   Stealing cars now.

ADAM   Yep.

MAN   Typical fucking Tottenham fan.

            Beat.

            You laughed.

ADAM   I didn't laugh.

MAN   You fucking did.

ADAM   I ditch the car near to the church and walk quickly down the road.

            I walk through the grounds and see people walking out already.

            I'm late.

I'm always late.

Out of time.

I turn into the graveyard and I can see her.

By the headstone.

Alone.

I want to hug her.

Say something.

But what is there to say.

LILY   If it was my –

ADAM   Well it's not okay. It's not your parents. It's not your *oh-so-fucking-perfect* family. So don't tell me what I have to think. What I have to do.

LILY   I wasn't. I wasn't, Adam.

ADAM   I'm going to the pub.

        He moves to leave.

        Stops.

        Oh fuck.

LILY   What?

ADAM   I'm him.

LILY   Who?

ADAM   I'm just the same as fucking him.

LILY   Adam, what are you –

ADAM   My father.

        I.

        We.

        Us.

        We are so connected.

LILY   No, no you're not.

ADAM   A connection.

LILY   You're not, Adam.

ADAM   A name.

LILY   Don't say that.

ADAM   A vein collapses.

        A monitor flatlines.

        A door closes.

        Or does it open.

MAN   There were good times, you know. As well as bad.

ADAM   Yeah. I know.

MAN   I am sorry.

ADAM   You shouldn't say that unless you mean it.

MAN   I do. Your turn now.

ADAM   To you? Fuck off.

MAN   No. To your mam.

WOMAN   You didn't need to come.

ADAM   I did.

WOMAN   I texted you.

ADAM   I know.

WOMAN   You didn't reply.

ADAM   I didn't know what to do.

        A silence.

WOMAN   He was an arsehole.

ADAM   Yeah. He was.

WOMAN   But he was still your dad.

ADAM   I thought...

WOMAN   What?

ADAM   I wish I had come. Sooner. I wish I'd seen him before he –

WOMAN   Shhh.

         The WOMAN *hugs* ADAM.

         You're here. Now. That's what matters.

                              ***

MATTY *is reading his phone.*

TATE *is looking at* MATTY.

TATE   Is that him then?

MATTY   Yeah.

TATE   What's he saying?

MATTY   Saying he's late.

TATE   Yeah.

MATTY   Going to be a bit later.

TATE   How much later?

MATTY   Doesn't say.

TATE   Shit. My arse is clapping in the cold.

         Beat.

         Is there more?

MATTY   Yeah.

TATE   Long message.

MATTY   Says have we remembered our cash and equipment.

TATE   What does he mean, 'cash and equipment'?

MATTY   I don't know.

TATE   I don't have any cash and equipment.

MATTY   I know.

TATE   Fucking cash for what?

MATTY   Tate, I don't know. I'm just...

TATE   Reply and ask him what.

MATTY   I am doing. Will you give me fucking chance?

Beat.

Got to get the wording right. Don't want to get bollocked.

TATE   I'll fucking bollock him. Round the head, bang bang, each bollock.

MATTY   He'll eat your bollocks, mate.

MATTY *is still typing.*

TATE   Right lot of shit this is. Right lot of proper shit.

MATTY   I think he means painting and decorating equipment.

TATE   What like brushes and that?

MATTY   Yeah.

TATE   Course we haven't got brushes. Brushes? Who does he think we are? Fucking Basil Brush and, and Ian Brush? Did you tell him we had our own equipment?

MATTY   No. I just presumed he'd have it all.

TATE   I mean, you don't expect you have to take your own pens to school when you're a teacher. Your dad doesn't expect to take his own dildos to the dildo factory, does he? Hey?

Beat.

Hey?

MATTY   I've text him.

TATE   What did you say?

MATTY   I just asked what he meant.

TATE   Yeah but what did you actually say?

MATTY   Does it matter?

TATE	Yeah, it does fucking matter because so far I've left all this to you and we're sat in the middle of nowhere waiting for a nasty painter and decorator who's expecting us to have fucking money, paint and buckets for him.
MATTY	I've said 'no problem mate, what equipment and cash sorry'.
TATE	Sorry?
MATTY	Yeah. Like sorry for the confusion.
TATE	Not our fault though, is it?
MATTY	No, but /
TATE	/ Unless he did tell you and you forgot.
MATTY	No, he didn't tell me.
TATE	So then it's his fucking fault and he should be the one saying sorry.
MATTY	Ah man, you can't talk to him like that. He'd skin your arse.
TATE	But I'm not talking to him, am I? I'm talking to you.

Silence.

Fucking cash. Cash for what? He's meant to be the one paying us.

| MATTY | I don't know, do I? |

Beat.

Like, petrol money or something. Rent. I don't know.

| TATE | Fucking hell, mate. You've stitched us up here, haven't you? |

Pause.

| MATTY | You keep saying that but you can fuck off if you want to. |
| TATE | Can I? |

MATTY   Yeah.

TATE   I'm allowed to fuck off? You've given me
          permission?

MATTY   Yes, you can fuck off. And you can fuck yourself
          while you're doing it.

TATE   What, fuck myself while I'm fucking off? Like
          walking down the road fucking myself?

MATTY   Yeah.

TATE   I wouldn't be able to reach around.

MATTY   Well then you can use one of them branches then,
          can't you?

TATE   Well if I use a branch then I'm not fucking myself,
          am I? I'm being fucked by a branch. Think about
          your wording, Matty. It can obviously get you into
          a right lot of shit.

          Pause.

          TATE *sits down.*

MATTY   So you're staying then.

TATE   Looks it, doesn't it?

MATTY   Yeah.

          Beat.

TATE   Has he responded?

MATTY   No.

          Beat.

TATE   We'll just have to tell him that we didn't know.

          Beat.

          We'll just have to tell him that we didn't know and
          we're sorry and we'll sort something out when we
          get there. I mean, that's fine. That should be fine
          with him. He's a businessman, a man of business.

          Pause.

We just get to London and we do this job and we get some money and find our own place and then we're done. We're sorted. This is nothing, this is easy mode. This is bugger-all compared to the shit at home.

MATTY   Do you mean Jenny?

TATE   I mean everything. More than just... See, the Jenny thing pisses me off because everyone presumes that because it's a big deal for her it means it's got to be a big deal for me. Well, you know what, it just isn't. Sorry. It isn't.

MATTY   Maybe it's meant to.

TATE   How would you know?

Beat.

MATTY   Maybe I don't know about that but I do know about running away from something.

Beat.

And it never lasts, mate. You need to have something to go to rather than just something to get away from. It's the only way that leaving can work.

TATE   Do you mean when you lived in Manchester?

MATTY   A bit. And you can manage for long enough but without something to grip on to, something that's pulling you towards it, then eventually something just...

TATE   Just what?

MATTY   Something happens to you, you get a sign, that tells you that you don't belong.

TATE   You get a sign?

MATTY   Yeah.

TATE   Like what? Written down?

MATTY   It can be anything.

TATE   What was it for you?

MATTY   A person.

TATE   Like an angel?

MATTY   No. Darker than that.

TATE   Like what?

MATTY   You know, I was staying in that cheap-as-shit house
I was telling you about. It had this weird landlady.
Real creepy woman with a face like chicken skin.
I thought it was just me and her for ages. I was there
for near on a month before I saw this bloke, this odd
bloke who was staying there too. I never heard him,
she never mentioned him. But one morning I was
on my way to this scrapping job with our lad and
I passed this neighbour on the stairs, this real slinky
weirdo that always had a shadow over him. He was
just coming in and I thought well that's funny. It's
first thing and he's coming in. I said hello. I tried to
be friendly, but he said nothing back, he just looked
at me. He looked at me with these rolling eyes
coming out of the shadows. And he…

TATE   He what?

MATTY   It's just… He started to… Thing is, he started to…
He begun to knock on my door. At night. I mean
he'd come up to my room and knock on my door
like a fucking right weirdo. Three or four knocks,
that was it. Enough to scare the life out of me. Shat
my pants every night.

TATE   Fucking hell. What did you do?

MATTY   I didn't know what I could do… I never said
anything, I'd just sit there frozen. I should've said.
I should've said to the landlady but I was worried
because I thought I might lose the deposit. And so
it kept going. And every night he'd knock on my
door and frighten me stiff. Knock. Knock. Knock.
And I'd sit there thinking hello what the bloody
hell am I doing here. Is this really worth all this
shit? And I don't know why. I don't know why but
it had just driven me so crazy this fucking cunt

knocking and so one night I just… answered the
door. I answered the door.

TATE   What happened?

MATTY   He he pushed me into the room… and he hit me.
And he ripped my shirt right across my chest like
that and he hit me twice in the mouth. He didn't…
He didn't say a word. He just hit me.

Pause.

And he just stood there. And it felt weird, not just
the punching and that. I mean him there, in my
space, my room, where I sleep, near all my stuff.
He was like a cancerous cell in an organ or
something. And then he just left. He left my room
and left me to close my door.

TATE   Fuck.

MATTY   Yeah.

TATE   Manchester.

MATTY   Yeah.

Beat.

And for a moment that room was the quietest
place I've ever been. And I knew. That was my sign.
I knew I didn't belong. I knew I had to come home.

MATTY*'s phone goes again.*

***

ADAM   Hey.

LILY   Hey?!

ADAM   Yeah. Hey.

LILY   Where the fuck are you I've been going out of my
mind.

ADAM   I'm sorry.

I mean it.

I really do.

He died.

LILY   Adam…

ADAM   Can you come and meet me?

LILY   Yes. Of course. Where are you?

ADAM   And the word feels strange when I say it, but right.

Home.

LILY   Are you okay?

A silence.

Adam?

ADAM   And I think.
I take a moment…
And I think.
And it feels like the first time in an age.
And around me I can see trees.
And fields.
And houses.
And people.
And no roads.
Or traffic.
Or shops.
Or wankers dressed like me playing with their
iPhones or checking their Facebooks or tweeting or
taking a selfie or –

I shut my eyes. Take a breath. And let it drop.

The amputation of a limb.

The loss of a parent.

The conversation as we part.

The fading light.

An ending. A beginning. A new.

An ending.

A beginning.

A new.

LILY   Adam…

ADAM   We are so connected.

So connected.

So far apart.

LILY   Adam, you're scaring me…

ADAM   Yes.

I am.

Or at least I will be.

When you get here.

I'll be alright then.

***

MATTY *is reading a text.*

TATE   So what's he saying?

MATTY   He says it's money for the van. Says it's five hundred.

TATE   Five hundred quid?

MATTY   Yeah.

TATE   Fuck off. What on a van costs five hundred quid, unless he doesn't actually have a van himself… Does he have a van or is he buying it?

MATTY   I dunno mate, do I?

TATE   Fuck me.

MATTY   I'm texting him now.

TATE   Right lot of shit this is.

MATTY   He says he's got enough equipment and he's got our room and everything, we just need to shout him for the van.

TATE   He could have told us before we left the house.

MATTY   Yeah, I know.

TATE   Text him and ask him why he couldn't let us know that it's five hundred for the van before we left the fucking house.

MATTY   I'm not texting him that.

TATE   Then I'll text him that.

MATTY   You do that then he'll fuck you in the mouth when he sees you. I told you, you've got to be careful.

TATE   Shit.

           MATTY*'s phone goes again.*

MATTY   Here. He's saying we can owe him for the van. Pay him when we're done.

TATE   Five hundred though. That's half our money for the job.

MATTY   Yeah.

TATE   It'd be like one of us working for free.

MATTY   Yeah.

           Beat.

TATE   Do you trust him?

MATTY   I don't know. He's a bit random.

           Beat.

TATE   But what else can we do?

           A phone buzzes.

           It's TATE*'s.*

MATTY   You could start by sorting that out.

TATE   That has got nothing to do with this.

MATTY   It's got everything to do with it, mate.

TATE   You don't understand.

MATTY   I don't even mean for her sake. I mean for mine.
          I need to know if you're just running away because
          if you are then it's not going to last and that's going
          to leave me in the shit. I can't have a Manchester
          happen to me again, I just can't.

TATE   I'm going because I want to go to London. It's got
          nothing to do with here.

MATTY   You're not running away?

TATE   No.

          TATE*'s phone goes again.*

MATTY   What if that's it, what if that's your sign?

TATE   My what?

MATTY   Your sign telling you that you shouldn't be going,
          that you don't belong in London?

TATE   Because it's bullshit, Matty. I don't believe in that.

MATTY   You don't believe in a lot, do you, Tate?

          His phone goes again.

TATE   What if it's not my phone, what if it's this fucking
          nasty bloke delaying us and demanding money.
          That's more of a sign than a, a...

MATTY   Baby?

          TATE *sits on the floor.*

          How was she when she told you?

TATE   Angry.

MATTY   Yeah.

TATE   We weren't even together for long.

MATTY   Long enough.

TATE   Fuck off.

MATTY   True though.

TATE   You know, yes, you're right. I've never left home like you have. I've never worked with a nasty scrapper, I've never rented a room, I've never done anything like that. But what's different, Matty, is that I've got a proper, proper, proper reason to leave. And maybe, just maybe, that's strong enough to keep me gone.

Headlights shine on TATE *and* MATTY.

MATTY   Look.

TATE   Do you reckon it's him?

MATTY   Who else would it be?

TATE   Right. Yeah.

MATTY   So are we doing it then? Hey? Are we doing it, mate?

End.

MAISIE SAYS SHE LOVES ME

a monologue

Jimmy Osborne

This one's for HS, the Big Man and the Bear

Maisie Says She Loves Me was first performed at VAULT Festival, London, on 1 March 2017, directed and performed by David Aula.

Jimmy and David make theatre together as Aula & Osborne – @aula_osborne & aulaosbornetheatre.com

Design by NB Studio
Original music by Corasandel
Original show artwork by Lee Conybeare

Thanks to Craig Morrow and the Lincoln Performing Arts Centre for development and support. Paines Plough and their Roundabout. Mat Burt, Andy George, Tim Wilson, Josh Morrell & all at VAULT Festival. Nick Finney, Alan Dye, Jamie Beach, Saphira Parry & Hannah Rea at NB Studio for design and adventures. Simon Evans for early direction. Mel and Suzi at Badger Farm. Mark Merrifield for sonics. Matt Applewhite & Sarah Liisa Wilkinson at Nick Hern Books. Julie Press at Kitson Press Associates.

Character

SHELDON, *male, thirty years old*

SHELDON. I always wanted a family. A big one. I know
you're only supposed to have two kids these days, so we
don't mess up the planet any more than it's already messed
up. Two of you to make two kids, and then when you both
die you cancel them out – no-score draw. I know that is
what you are supposed to do, but I always wanted this
massive family. One of those families where you're not sure
how many actual children there are. Everything a blur of
movement. A house full of kids careering around. All this
laughter and chaos and noise. Noise. When I was a kid our
house was so quiet. Like it was empty. The house made
more noise than we did. Squeaking doors. Gurgling pipes.
Creaking stairs. I memorised which stairs creaked: the third,
seventh and ninth. That way I always missed them. I never
made any noise. Never drew attention to myself. The house
was always so quiet. Mostly.

Quiet. I think more people should value peace and quiet.
Everyone seems to move so fast. Everyone always talks about
how busy they are. Everyone seems to be waiting for that time
when 'things quieten down'. I think people should work
harder to find that quiet themselves. If more people did then
I think the world would be a better, safer place. Wars are
started by busy people who can't relax. When I need peace
and quiet I go down to the lakes outside of town. I cast my
line and I cast and reel, cast and reel while my mind relaxes.
I know some like to fish in the canals, or they set up on the
banks of the river through town, but that does not seem right
to me. Fishing with the sound of cars charging past. Setting up
amongst the crisp packets and Coke cans. Fishing should be
out in the countryside. It's worth the drive. Only you and the
water. What are you going to catch in town? Condoms and
traffic cones. Where is the peace in that? Where is the quiet?

Maisie laughs at me sometimes. When I stay at her place.
She says she never hears me moving around the flat. I just
appear quietly in a room. Like a ghost. She turns round and
I'm there. Makes her jump. I like making her jump. She does

this little squeal. Half-delighted, half-afraid. Makes me smile. When I've made her jump Maisie likes me to hold her close so I can feel her heart beating fast. That's the effect I have on her, so she says. I don't know whether it's delight or fear. Sometimes I can't tell which I'd prefer it to be. I like Maisie. She wants lots of kids too. With me apparently. She told me this late one night after too much Chablis. That's her drink. You pay over the odds for the name, she says, but she likes it best. She always wants me to try some, but I never do. I don't like to drink. Maisie'd had nearly a bottle to herself when she blurted it out: 'I'd love to have kids with you, like five or six little Sheldons and Maisies. I'd love it.' I was shocked. We'd only been seeing each other six months. That's very soon to be talking about children. I was shocked, and for a moment very happy. Maisie thought she'd scared me off, that I'd 'do a runner'. Apparently you don't mention children to a man until you've been together for at least a year. That's the rule she says. I told her it was okay. I wanted a big family. I could see our house together in that moment. See all the Maisies and Sheldons flying up and down the stairs. Hear all the 'Daaaaad!' The rustle of Lego. The quiet of bedtime stories. In that fraction of a second I thought of all the great books I would read them. The books I have loved that I might help them find. All the stories that could colour their dreams. I imagined standing in their bedrooms later at night when they are asleep. Listening to them breathing, just so I know that they're alive. They're asleep and they are happy – the world is well. I told Maisie that it was okay, I won't run, and she gave me her best smile, like a pinball machine lighting up. I felt warm all over.

I did not want to hurt her.

I have one sister. We are not close any more. Birthday and Christmas cards et cetera. We see each other when someone dies, when someone is born or someone gets married. My sister calls every few months to see if I'm okay. That's nice of her, but it feels like someone ringing up to find out if my washing machine is still working properly. A contractual obligation. I like her, my sibling. She is a nice person. We don't argue or fight. We never say a cross word to each other. We are simply not close. It happens. Sometimes being family

gets in the way. Maisie wanted to meet her. I did not think
that this was a good idea. We are not close, I told her. 'But
she's your sister, I've got to meet her!' She kept on asking
and asking, and I said no. I was reasonable. There is no need
for those parts of my life to meet if I do not want them to,
but Maisie would ask again. Family is important to her so
she does not understand. I said no again, and she asked
again. It was like being prodded around until you do what
you're told. Always asking.

Beat.

(*Snarls.*) 'I said no, are you deaf!'

Beat.

I shouldn't have snapped at her. That was wrong. It was the
first time I shouted at her. She stood there and looked at me
for a moment, before looking away. I immediately regretted
it. I do not want Maisie to think bad of me. Some of that
warmth I felt left me, but only some. I was very apologetic.
I bought her a bottle of Chablis bordering on the expensive.
I kept apologising until she told me that it was forgotten.
Maisie is a very forgiving woman. It is one of her many
endearing qualities. If we'd had children I hope that they
would have inherited that from her. Children need
forgiveness in them. You become so disappointed in your
parents. They start off as these gods. All-knowing. All-
powerful. Then time breaks them down before your eyes
into these confused, tired, sad and pathetic creatures. Where
you once saw a giant in control of the world, you finally see
that they understand even less about this life than you. The
world has left them behind. It was a relief when mine were
both dead. It was like they'd set me free. I do not mark their
birthdays or deathdays. I don't raise a toast to 'Mum and
Dad' at Christmas. My father would not approve of me
making a toast with water in any case. They are gone. My
sister and I never talk about our parents. I cannot tell if this
is because we are not close, or why we are not close.
Whatever the reason, the words will not come out.

I go out to the lakes. I need the peace and quiet. Maisie and
I are fine, but I feel something. It is like the rumbling of a train

passing nearby, but there is no train out here at the lakes. Only me and the water. Nothing really bites, a few little things, nothing worth putting in the record book. My mind does not want to calm, but I cast and reel, cast and reel, cast and reel, and eventually I am almost at peace. I shouldn't be. I know coming out to fish is odd, but sometimes if something works you have to just do it and not fill your head with the questions that want to gnaw at you. Coming here to the water works. Yes, yes, it works. I cannot be weak. I will not be weak.

Maisie's parents are very loving people. Their house is always warm. It glows inside. This is why Maisie makes me feel so warm. She visits her parents often. I regularly make excuses not to go, but it makes her happy that I am there so occasionally I go with her. It is important to me that Maisie is happy. Her parents love a 'get-together'. They are keen to have people around them. They have aunties and uncles and cousins and nieces and nephews always popping round for a 'get-together'. When we are there it is a constant stream of people having cups of tea, or cake or wine. Henry, Maisie's dad, is a twenty-four-hour waiter, constantly serving drinks, moving from person to person, laughter following him. He drinks red wine. He seems to drink quite a lot of red wine, but he is always smiling and kind, if a little bleary-eyed and clumsy. There are faded patches of red here and there on their sofa. The worst that happens is if he ever sits down he'll nod off and begin to snore. I was worried that he would not like me because I do not drink. I find that not drinking often makes the people around me awkward when they are drinking. They seem to think that I am making a judgement about them. As if my orange juice disapproves of their real ale. It looks down its nose at their Pinot Grigio. It thinks their vodka and Coke is 'common'. It does not. My orange juice is not the slightest bit interested in what other people are drinking. But no one seems to notice that. They seem to be affronted that I do not join in. 'Just have one.' No. 'Go on, I'll get you one.' No, thank you. 'Let go for once, Sheldon.' Let go. Let go. Everyone rushes to let go without thinking about what might happen. Although, I suppose if you wondered about what might happen, then that would not really be letting go. I stopped going to the pub with people from work a long time ago because of this. I seemed to be spoiling their fun. They were much happier without me.

Henry doesn't mind though. 'Each to their own,' is his motto.
When he sees me he says that more people should be like me.
I am not so sure about that. Henry thinks the world would be a
better place if people drank less. He says this while opening
bottles of Cabernet Sauvignon and pouring huge glasses that
you could do the backstroke in. Their house is full of laughter.
This is what I would like my house to be like, but for some
reason, I find it hard to see all this happiness. When I go there,
I regularly have to lock myself in the toilet for a few moments
so that I can catch my breath. Maisie's mum, Audrey, always
jokes that I have a weak bladder. I do not. Her joke can irritate
me, but she is not being mean. It is important that I remember
that Audrey is not being mean to me. Maisie's parents are very
loving people.

I used to go fishing with my father when I was young. He
liked to fish. When he caught a trout and brought it home for
dinner he would be so pleased with himself. My mother
hated gutting the creature, but she always made a good job of
it. When he fished my father seemed happy. He would let me
prepare the bait. He taught me how to pierce the worm with
the hook. My father was very particular. He drummed it into
me that it must be right. I never really liked fishing then, but
I loved being with him by the water. It was the place where
he seemed most like my father. He only drank tea from a
flask when he fished. When I was ten years old my father
bought me my own fishing rod. He seemed to want me to be
there with him. Told me that he was taught to fish by his
father. It was passed down from father to son, father to son.

Maisie says she loves me. When she tells me this she has a
look on her face like she's at peace with the world.
Connected to the planet and the people and the air and every
damn atom of this Earth. Maisie says she loves me. I like
Maisie. No. I really like her. I am bordering on love.
Hovering round the edges. I keep trying to go the whole way.
I can see what it would be like. What Maisie and I would be
like if I flew into it wholeheartedly, but every time I decide
to do it I can't seem to… like a stupid moth forever banging
its head against a window pane. Never realising that for all its
fluttering and effort it will not get though. Maisie does not
worry that I do not say that I love her back. She says that she

can see it in me. I do not like to think that someone can see
something in me that I am not sure I feel. It seems
presumptuous on their part. But perhaps... maybe I do, but
I do not recognise it. I suffer from indigestion, but maybe it is
not indigestion. Maybe it is love? I am not sure so I will keep
taking the antacid tablets and stay away from curries. Maisie
loves me so much that she asked me to move in with her. Her
flat is bigger than mine. I intentionally live in a small flat. That
way it is easier to keep it neat. Ordered. Living with Maisie
would not be like that. She is a very relaxed person. Maisie
would never start a war. She can never find any of her things
without pulling the whole place apart. This would drive me
mad. Mad. I would be concerned for my books. I have my
books ordered in a very particular way. Most people, if they
are organised enough, order their books alphabetically by
author surname. The more extreme ones will then break it
down further into fiction, non-fiction, poetry, travel writing
and so on. Like bookshops in their house. I believe that these
people are show-offs. They want you to know how intelligent
they are. They want you to be in awe of the breadth of their
knowledge. I do not subscribe to this method. A book on a
shelf is public thing even in your own home. So I order my
books by the colour of the cover. They look beautiful, a
rainbow of stories across the shelves. I do not want anyone to
think I am clever. I want them to think about how wonderful
the books are. This is why, although I like technology, a book
cannot be digital for me. It has to exist in the real world to
show its true colour. To be held. A physical doorway to a room
that I can forget myself in for a time. This system would not
last three minutes with Maisie. She would not even have to
pick a book up before the whole thing somehow fell apart.
No, it would not be a good idea to live together. I tell Maisie
that I like things as they are. We are happy. She thinks that it is
because I am tidy and she is messy. Maisie wants to prove to
me that she can be tidy. Her flat becomes suspiciously tidy, but
I can tell that it is that special kind of tidy where someone has
rushed around before you arrive so that you do not think they
are messy. It is not tidying. It is hiding. The mess is still there,
undercover, waiting to be discovered. It is not the kind of tidy
that would last day in, day out. You cannot hide from someone
when you live with them. Maisie can tell that this is not

changing my mind. So one day when I am at work she lets
herself into my flat and cleans it. Cleans every inch of it. It is
already clean. Very clean. I am the one who cleaned it. When
I come home from work she is there waiting for me. She is
smiling. There are books that are...

Beat – SHELDON *wrings his hands.*

(*Low.*) Nothing is where it should be. These are my things,
you stupid cow! Get out!

Beat.

Maisie is on the floor of the landing outside my flat, she holds
her arm where I hauled her out. She says later that she tripped
as I pushed her out of the door. She says she tripped. I cannot
remember if she tripped or if I pushed her. I think... I think
maybe I pushed... but she said, she said that she tripped. She
landed close to the top of the stairs. I think about what would
have happened if she had fallen down them.

It takes me most of the weekend to put my flat right. It's not
just a case of moving a few things around. I have to start at
the beginning. To make sure that it is all as it should be. To
make it mine again. At least it occupies my mind. Gives me
something to focus on... because the phone does not ring.

Maisie and I have no contact with each other for three days.
I go to see her. I am more apologetic this time. I buy her two
bottles of expensive Chablis. I do not feel as warm as I once
did. I tell her that I am under lots of pressure at work. I am
not under pressure at work. I find my job very easy. Lying is
not something I like to do to Maisie. She is very trusting.
This is because of her very loving family. Maisie tells me
that I must control my temper. I tell her that it will never
happen again. She says that maybe I should talk to someone.
(*Laughs.*) Talk to someone! Like my car's got a problem.
I do not need to talk to anyone. She keeps saying maybe
I do. She keeps putting 'maybe' in front of everything she
says. 'Maybe' – she doesn't want to set me off. I can tell that
she is trying to not make me angry and it makes me so...
because I am not weak! I am not. I swear to her that it will
never happen again. I beg her to believe me. I promise all
these things. I know she wants to believe me. She loves me.

You believe the people you love, don't you? So I promise
and promise, and say these things softly. I move slowly
towards her. She isn't sure, but I keep moving slowly
towards Maisie, speaking softly so that she will believe me.
I can see she wants to believe me. I can see it, so I hold on to
that. If she wants to believe then she will. I just mustn't do
this too fast or too hard, I have to do this just right, and she
will believe me.

Pause.

Eventually, I hold her close to me and can feel her heart
beating very fast.

My father bought me my own fishing rod one weekend when
I was ten years old. He presented it to me like it was the most
important gift in the world. I did my best to look suitably
honoured and thankful. I was thankful, truly, but I felt the
pressure of the gift. The expectation. I did not know if I could
live up to what my father wanted me to be. Later that day we
went fishing. My hands trembled as I prepared to cast my first
line. My father spotted it. 'A man does not shake, boy.' I did
my best to push it down inside myself, to not let anything
show, to please him. I cast the line and I waited. And I prayed
for something to happen. I prayed. I prayed to whichever gods
may be listening to a ten-year-old boy, standing in the cold
with a fishing rod. Nothing. I cast again and wait. And I wait.
My hands don't want to shake any more, my whole arms want
to quake now. I try to tense them, to hold it in, I try to relax
them, to let it go. Anything I can think of. There is an itch on
my nose. It begins small and slight, perhaps not really there,
but then it grows and grows so that I am desperate to scratch
it, but I dare not take my hands off the rod. The itch consumes
my entire face, but I do not let go of the rod. I will not betray
myself. The gods aren't listening, so I call out to anything my
little mind can think of. I call out to the universe itself to
please, please do something for me. No matter how small I
am. No matter how insignificant. Please do something. Please.
Now. And then – ah! A faint flicker of ripples near my float.
A shadow moves under the water. The float bobs, the line tugs
once, then twice. The universe has spoken. A catch! A catch!
It may only have been a small river, but that fish on my line
felt like a marlin! The way it pulled at me, struggled, the way

it tried to break free. I reeled it in like my father had taught me, not too fast or hard, but not too slow. I reeled it in just right. My father and I marvelled at the fish. I had caught a two-and-half-pound trout. It was this big! My father was so proud. I thought that I could see tears in his eyes. This would be our dinner. He made me kill the fish by beating it on the head once, hard, with a small wooden mallet he kept especially for this. Its eyes were bulging as I raised the mallet.

Beat.

Despite my excitement I did not like killing the fish, but I wanted my father to be happy with me.

Things are awkward between Maisie and myself for a couple of weeks. I apologised and she accepted that, but she keeps her distance a little. We talk on the phone. We go for dinner. I stay over at hers a couple of times, she doesn't stay over at mine. It is not what it was. I apologised. What more does she want from me? Someone apologises and you get back to normal. That is how it is supposed to work, but there is something there between us, I can feel it. It does not come from me. It's her, she is doing this to us. She is polite. She does not act upset or angry, but there is something there. When I ask her what's wrong, she says, 'Nothing', but that is not true. She lies to me about it. She wants me to feel bad. So bad that I will agree to move in with her. She thinks that I do not see this. She thinks that she is being clever. That I will be too stupid to work out what she is doing, but I know, I know. I act like I have not noticed. Eventually she will realise that her plan will not work. And I will not be so annoyed with her.

My father could not wait to get home to show my mother the fish that I had caught. We packed up our tackle and strode purposefully to the car. I felt like I had been tested, and that I had proven myself to be worthy. My father had his hand on my shoulder. A proud hand. It was nice to feel his touch. It was warm. His strong fingers held on to me, almost became a part of me. We chatted excitedly about how Mum should cook the fish. I said fried. My father said baked, with lemon and herbs. We agreed that she should bake it with lemon and herbs. In that moment I was happier than I had ever been. Which is why, when I tripped up, it was so unfair.

I should not think about Maisie like that. She is kind. She is
thoughtful. She is loving. She does not do things to annoy me.
Not deliberately. She does not plan to hurt me. She wants to
have a family with me. I should not think about Maisie like
that. I go to the lake out of town... and I cast and reel, cast and
reel, cast and reel, cast and reel, cast and reel, cast and... it
does not work like it once did. Why does it not work? I want
my mind to be quiet, but there is this constant... chatter... like
static in my brain. I can't think clearly to decide what to do.
The noise of it echoing in my skull. Makes my head burn.
I stay there for hours in the rain, this pounding rain that drives
anyone else fishing home, but I stay.

Pause.

When I tripped I was carrying my new fishing rod. As I fell
I landed on it, snapping it clean in two. Pride in my father's
eyes was replaced by a rush of blood filling the whites. He
didn't say a word. Simply hauled me to my feet. Dragged me
to the car. Unlocked it. Opened the door. Placed my left hand
on the passenger doorframe and slammed the door on my
fingers. He broke three. Then he threw me in the car with
rest of the tackle and drove home. My mother was forced to
gut and cook the fish before being allowed to take me to
hospital. He had hurt me before. And my sister. And my
mum. But as I clutched my white-hot hand in the corner of
the kitchen, with the room full of the stench of fish, lemon,
dill and parsley, I decided that I would not allow it any more.
The universe would not help me. I could not rely on my
mum. She tried to protect us, I know, and maybe she stopped
some of it. But she had no control. At the hospital she said
that the wind blew the kitchen door on to my hand. I realised
that it was up to me.

I have never had lots of girlfriends. Not drinking and not
having a girlfriend are two of the things that pretty much
mark you out as seriously strange to lots people. You are not
ticking the right boxes on what a human being should be and
do. That is not to say that I did not want relationships. That I
did not desire someone. There were nights, sat on the sofa in
my flat, where I could almost feel someone sat next to me,
and I thought about stepping outside and going to find
someone to be with. There must be someone out there in all

of the world for me, but I did not think it was a good idea.
I have had brief liaisons from time to time. I am human after
all, but I never thought that a long-term relationship was for
me. Until I met Maisie. There was something about her.
Something I wanted to keep hold of. I knew it would end
badly, only I could not say no.

I waited until the next time my father was hurting one of us.
I did not have to wait long. My fingers were still in splints.
At dinner one night my sister knocked her orange juice over.
A little thing. A tiny thing that happens a millions times
around the world to a million people every day. Such a small
thing that should not matter. All it takes is a cloth and half a
minute and it is dealt with. That is all it takes. She knew
what was coming and ran up to her room, hitting the third,
seventh and ninth stairs as she fled. Each creak a countdown
to the explosion that was coming. My father followed while
Mum occupied herself cleaning up the mess. I was very fond
of my sister. There were times when I would ask her to come
into my room, and I would read stories to her. To show her
all these other lives that were out there. All these other lives
different to ours. That one day we might have lives like
them. She didn't seem to believe it, not like I used to believe
it back then. She listened, though. I like to think that that was
a good thing, but I could never tell. A quiet little girl, like we
were all quiet. I did not like hearing her being hurt. So I went
to her room and found my father with his belt off. Welts
covered the back of my sister's legs. She was seven.

'Get out, boy.'

No.

'Out or you'll be next.'

No.

He advances on me. This simmering mass of rage. Trembling
as the energies locked within his body desperately try to
break out into the world. I already knew what I would do. I
had a plan. My hands only shook a little, as I backed out on
to the landing outside the bedroom, smiling to get him to
follow me out there.

'Don't laugh at me, child.'

I did not feel like a child. It was as if I had become this
other thing, a different being. That to do what I needed to
do I couldn't remain simply Sheldon. I did not feel scared
even as he raised the belt. I only marvelled at how much his
eyes bulged. I pushed him hard, surprised by how strong my
ten-year-old arms could be. My broken fingers screamed at
me, but I did not care. He tumbled down the stairs over and
over and over.

When he hit the bottom I sat and watched his pain for a little
while.

I am causing Maisie pain by not moving in with her. Moving
in with each other is what normal people do. It is normal.
Maisie is making me feel bad. She has no right to make me
feel like this. I am trying. I am trying and she makes me feel...
no, no I will not allow this. Remember Maisie. Maisie Says
She Loves Me. Maisie Says She Loves Me. I must be strong.
She is kind and wonderful. I must be strong... but she twists
all the thoughts up inside me, she forces me to be like this.
It's not my fault, it's not... Maisie Says She Loves Me, Maisie
Says She Loves Me, Maisie Says She Loves Me. I must be
vigilant with my thoughts. I must not let them out. I must be
strong. I must push them down and fight them. I will not allow
myself to be weak. Remember, remember, Sheldon. Maisie
just wants to be with me. I should remember this. Maisie
wants to be with me. Me.

I go and see Maisie. I have been unkind to her. I want to tell
her this. That I care about her. That she is the only person
who has made me want to be with her. We have been
together eighteen months. I take flowers. Not the cliché of
roses, but lilies, iris and daisies. In the florist's they look big
and bright, stood at her doorstep they look shrivelled and
pathetic and suddenly I cannot remember if she likes flowers
or not. She does not go for chocolates and perfume, she is
not like that. Then why have I bought flowers? Stupid,
stupid! And the door opens. She seems surprised to find me
there with flowers, and immediately I can tell that flowers
are not Maisie's thing, that I have known this all along, but
she takes them graciously. When I speak to her, my mouth
does not seem to work properly I trip over the words and the
sounds get 'stock' in my mouth. I stumble and grope my way

to saying that, 'I would like to move in with you. If you will still have me.' There is a fraction of a second between my words and her response that seems to last two ice ages. And then the old pinball smile returns and I want her so much. I feel warm again, like our home will be warm. Like our family will be warm and happy. Like I am happy. She reaches up to touch my face. I look down at her. I look down at her. I realise that it is not indigestion that I feel as I look down at Maisie. That the moth has finally broken through the window pane.

My father broke both his legs in the fall. I told my mum that if she did not move us away I would run away. She looked at me. I expected her to ask where I would go. I expected her to not believe a ten-year-old, but she looked into my eyes and she believed. We went to live with my gran. I never saw my father again. Even when he wrote that he was seriously ill. I decided it was best to let him die.

I look down at her. Maisie is precious. So alive. Remember this. Remember. She smiles at me and opens her mouth to speak. I do not want her to speak. Remember she is precious, Sheldon. Please do not do or say anything Maisie. Please. Not now. Let us be.

'I knew you would change your mind. You were being so silly, Sheldon.'

Silly? I am silly? The stupid little… presuming to know what I would do!

Long pause.

I did not want to hurt Maisie.

Long pause.

I did not want to hurt Maisie. So, so I tell her that we are over. Maisie says she loves me. Why am I doing this to her? I tell her it is over. I know that she will try and make me change my mind. I know that I do not think that I can resist that. So I tell her that moving in with her was a joke. 'Why would I move in with *you*? I don't feel anything for you. You have only been a way to waste some time.' Maisie wants to cry, I can tell, but she is strong, and she will not give me the satisfaction of seeing her cry. I marvel at how strong she is. I did not realise that she had all of that in her. How did I not see it before? I love her even more as I see her face set to stone. I can see that love of hers already turning to hate. And she yells a powerful, deep yell at me to get out. I obey her. I do not look back. I never go back. Never call. Never text. Maisie doesn't contact me ever again.

I am glad.

Pause.

I always wanted a big family. A really big one. Loads of kids. Loads. A house full of noise and laughter and warmth.

SHELDON *shivers.*

End.

Other Titles in this Series

www.nickhernbooks.co.uk

facebook.com/nickhernbooks

twitter.com/nickhernbooks